Richard Whitcombe is ITDG's Appropriate Technology Institutions Advisor responsible for the formulation, direction, execution and documentation of ITDG's work on the institutional aspects of appropriate technology. Previously he was ITDG's Africa Regional Advisor.

Dr. Marilyn Carr is an ITDG economist with special interest in the institutional aspects of appropriate technology. During 1975-8 she was seconded to the Economic Commission for Africa as an Expert in Village Technology with the African Research and Training Centre for Women.

Appropriate Technology Institutions: A Review
Richard Whitcombe and Marilyn Carr

Practical
ACTION
PUBLISHING

Practical Action Publishing Ltd
25 Albert Street, Rugby, CV21 2SD, Warwickshire, UK
www.practicalactionpublishing.com

© Intermediate Technology Publications 1982

First published 1982\Digitised 2008

ISBN 13 Paperback: 9781853391514
ISBN Library Ebook: 9781780441931
Book DOI: https://doi.org/10.3362/9781780441931

All rights reserved. No part of this publication may be reprinted or reproduced or utilized in any form or by any electronic, mechanical, or other means, now known or hereafter invented, including photocopying and recording, or in any information storage or retrieval system, without the written permission of the publishers.

A catalogue record for this book is available from the British Library.

The authors, contributors and/or editors have asserted their rights under the Copyright Designs and Patents Act 1988 to be identified as authors of their respective contributions.

Since 1974, Practical Action Publishing has published and disseminated books and information in support of international development work throughout the world. Practical Action Publishing is a trading name of Practical Action Publishing Ltd (Company Reg. No. 01159018), the wholly owned publishing company of Practical Action. Practical Action Publishing trades only in support of its parent charity objectives and any profits are covenanted back to Practical Action (Charity Reg. No. 247257, Group VAT Registration No. 880 9924 76).

Reasonable efforts have been made to publish reliable data and information, but the author and publisher cannot assume responsibility for the validity of all materials or for the consequences of their use.

ITDG wishes to acknowledge the contribution of the John Chataway who worked as research assistant on this study.

The manufacturer's authorised representative in the EU for product safety is Lightning Source France, 1 Av. Johannes Gutenberg, 78310 Maurepas, France.
compliance@lightningsource.fr

I. BACKGROUND AND CONTEXT OF THE REVIEW OF APPROPRIATE TECHNOLOGY INSTITUTIONS

The pioneers of the appropriate technology movement have, since its first development in the 1960s, brought the concept of AT into broad acceptance and to the forefront of development thinking. A considerable amount of research and development work has been undertaken in specific technologies, and it has become widely accepted that many technologies appropriate to the means and needs of the masses of the rural and urban poor in developing countries exist or could be developed.

There has been a dramatic increase in the number of institutions claiming interest and involvement in AT, particularly during the last five years. Centres and networks have been created to assist with the flow of AT information both between and within countries; efforts have been made to get existing research institutions to do more work on generating technologies of relevance to the rural and urban poor; specialized organizations have been started which are concerned solely with the generation or dissemination of AT; national committees have been set up to advise governments on AT, promoting the concept, and coordinating the activities of the agencies relevant to AT development and application; and many bilateral and multilateral aid agencies have become actively involved in encouraging and supporting AT initiatives of various kinds. Despite all this activity, however, little has happened in terms of widespread application of AT. Given this situation, the obvious question to be asked is whether these institutions are going the right way about achieving their 'common' long-term objectives and, if not, what is now needed to bring this about?

Until the mid-1970s, the appropriate technology movement saw its main task as that of promoting the concept of developing and disseminating technologies appropriate to the needs and circumstances of the poor in developing countries. It was hoped that the effectiveness of such technologies would in some way lead to changes in emphasis in aid programmes and development plans that would benefit all sections of society.

The pioneer AT institutions[1] focussed their efforts on encouraging the establishment of centres in the developing countries which could develop for themselves the ability to solve local problems with AT solutions. They would, it was hoped, thereby become more self-reliant and, in the process, create an awareness of the benefite among planners, administrators, entrepreneurs, university staff and other decision-makers. By the mid-1970s, there was a small but growing network of such AT centres, all of which hoped to bring about, eventually, funamental changes in the development process through practical example. Their work, and that of the handful of AT institutions in the developed countries, was carried out largely without the support of governments or international agencies.

In the second half of the 1970s, however the situation changed. Factors such as the worsening problems of unemployment and poverty in the developing countries, the oil crisis, and spiralling inflation, rising unemployment and worsening pollution in the developed countries of the West, brought a realization that alternatives were needed to capital-intensive, energy-intensive technologies which had little regard for either human needs or the environment. In 1973, Dr. E.F. Schumacher's **Small is Beautiful** encapsulated much of society's concern about these problems and offered, in appropriate technology, a potential solution. AT institutions began to spring up the world over: while there were only a handful in the early 1970s, there were over 500 in operation (of one form or another) by 1977, and an estimated 1,000 by 1980. This brought about a significant change in the nature of the appropriate technology movement.

Until the early 1970s, the few organizations in the AT movement had been working largely against the development establishment. Then, they were joined by the large international development agencies, aid administrations of developed countries, government ministries in developing countries, established centres of learning and research, and even some firms: all were increasingly interested in appropriate technology as an alternative means of tackling problems of unemployment and poverty in the Third World, or of opening up new markets in poor communities. The movement was also joined by various organizations primarily concerned with problems of the industrialized countries, such as ecology and energy.

The entry of these newcomers has been rather a mixed blessing, for although the AT movement has gained a degree of popularity and support that would have been difficult to imagine a decade ago, it has done so partly at the expense of losing some of its earlier focus on the needs and circumstances of the rural and urban poor in developing countries. In particular, many of the new organizations are concerned mainly with alternative energy technologies, many of which are inappropriate in terms of the needs, means and resources of the rural communities in developing countries. Even excluding such organizations, there is still a very mixed set of agencies which claim to be working on the implementation of truly appropriate technologies in developing countries. They include non-governmental organizations, universities, research and development institutes, developing country governments, aid administrations and international agencies – all of which have very different skills and resources to contribute to the work and, indeed, do so from different standpoints, perspectives and objectives.

While commercial enterprises, established R&D institutes, and others take care adequately of the development and dissemination of conventional 'western' technologies, they largely ignore the development and dissemination of technologies whose prospective beneficiaries are the poorer, weaker, less articulate sections of society whose needs and circumstances are very different and whose nature makes it almost impossible for them to exert any pressure through the market. There thus remains a need for catalytic agents which can assist the poorer sections of society to translate their needs into an effective demand for appropriate goods and services.

This catalytic process consists of several tasks: identifying needs and potential markets; seeking out appropriate technological solutions; adapting existing technologies or developing new ones to meet the needs; undertaking pilot operations to test processes or products under actual working conditions so as to iron out difficulties and to create an effective demand by demonstrating technical feasibility and economic viability; and transferring new processes and products to local entrepreneurs and rural users, complete with the technical and other support needed to ensure successful production and use.

In other words a complete hardware and software package has to be worked out for each technology in each circumstance. For the process to be successful, the intended beneficiaries, the rural and urban poor, will have to play an active role throughout. A variety of agencies will need to be involved in the provision of information, research and development and extension inputs. Government assistance will often be required through extension and by changing policies to facilitate the process.

The institutions involved in the AT movement all seek to play some part in this complicated process. Because of their variety in terms of country of location, size and budget, staff resources, and institutional affiliations, it has been far from easy for them to undertake all of these necessary tasks. Consequently, it has been difficult to ascertain what the particular role of each has been or what success each has had in achieving its own objectives.

There is currently very little literature on or detailed knowledge about AT institutions. A few institutions have written detailed accounts of specific aspects of their work, and a few institutional evaluations by outside agencies have been published.[2] However, attempts to collect and disseminate information about AT institutions have been largely limited to the compilation of directories based on answers to circulated questionnaires, supported by general documents put out by the institutions concerned. The largest of these directories are by UNEP (with 696 entries, of which about two-fifths are in the Third World), OECD (277 entries, about half Third World), and the Commonwealth Secretariat (131 entries from Commonwealth countries, about three-quarters Third World). A number of other organizations (including ILO, TRANET, VITA and the Canadian Freedom From Hunger Foundation) have published smaller, more selective lists, which do not claim to be comprehensive.[3]

Although such directories give an indication of the location and technical coverage of AT institutions, they have three major drawbacks. First, they give no real indication of the number of AT institutions in existence because: they include only those institutions which have received and responded adequately to a complicated questionnaire; they use varied criteria as to which institutions qualify as working on AT; and they become quickly out of date due to the high birth and death rates of such institutions.

Second, because they are based mainly on the responding agencies, expressed interest in AT, rather than on verified accounts of the impact that their work has had on the rural and urban poor, they give a confused and inflated idea of the actual activity in the field of appropriate technology. For example, the directories include many organizations which consider themselves active in the field merely because they are interested in rural problems. Others consider the technologies they generate are appropriate simply because for instance, they relate to solar or wind energy, even though their costs and other characteristics may place them beyond the reach of the poor of developing countries. Many are not engaged in the generation of appropriate technologies, but only in some related activities such as education or the provision of credit to small farmers and entrepreneurs. Others are small, informal groups with no operational links to research and development or extension networks, and with no capacity to generate or implement AT. To be fair, most of the compilers of directories have recognized this problem and some weeding out has been done. Nevertheless, the directories still contain a wide range of types of institutions without any concerted attempt to differentiate between them, and this is a major contributing factor to the current confusion about what an AT institution actually is.

Third, these directories tend to concentrate on an institution's involvement in particular technical subject areas, and give little or no information on how it has been established; how it is structured; how it works; what problems it has faced and how it has overcome them; and what assistance it needs and can use most effectively. This is not surprising, since it would be difficult to collect data through postal questionnaires and almost impossible to present it in directory form. Yet this is precisely the type of information that is now needed by groups and organizations wishing to set up an AT institution or to overcome difficulties in running an existing one — and is equally needed by governments, NGO's and aid agencies interested in providing support.

In recent years, ITDG has been receiving an increasing number of requests for information, advice and assistance of an institutional as opposed to a purely technical nature. Its experience of helping to set up AT institutions and of working with them has enabled it to respond to such requests in a limited way, but the ad hoc nature of this assistance is no longer adequate, and ITDG has been seeking ways in which to respond in a more structured way. It is believed that this study is an important step towards this objective.

The broad purpose of this study is therefore to review, classify and analyse the experience gained in the establishment and operation of AT institutions, to identify their purposes and objectives, strengths and weaknesses, achievements, and problems. This is seen as an essential initial step in clarifying some of the issues besetting the AT movement, identifying gaps in institutional knowledge, and providing institutional assistance. It is believed that such a comparative review can be used by both AT institutions themselves to examine themselves against the experiences of others, and by governments, NGOs and others who are planning to create or support AT institutions.

As there is little institutional information published, this study draws largely on AT institutions that are reasonably well known to ITDG. Within this constraint, institutions have been selected so as to give a reasonable geographical spread and to provide a good cross-section of experience and models (it is not claimed that no other models exist or that the best examples have necessarily been selected).

In all, some sixty AT institutions have been studied, of which three-quarters are located in developing countries. In addition, the institutional initiatives of bilateral and multilateral donor agencies, non-governmental organizations and other international agencies have been reviewed.[4] To analyse and draw conclusions from the experience of these institutions, it was necessary to categorize them in some meaningful way.[5] The institutions have been divided into three main categories: those located in the developing countries, those located in the developed countries, and international institutions. Each of these have been further sub-divided primarily on the basis of intended functions and/or institutional affiliation. AT institutions in developing countries, reviewed in Section II, are sub-divided into national appropriate technology committees, appropriate technology development centres, and regional institutions and initiatives: where appropriate, these are further divided into initiatives taken by governments, by universities and by NGOs. In developed countries, reviewed in Section III, the sub-division is into government centres, university initiatives, non-governmental centres, and other initiatives. The international institutions are reviewed on an agency-by-agency basis in Section IV. The overall findings are summarized and analysed in Section V, which also attempts to identify major gaps in existing institutional knowledge and to give some indication of the direction of further efforts.

II. APPROPRIATE TECHNOLOGY INSTITUTIONS IN DEVELOPING COUNTRIES

A variety of AT institutions are located in the developing countries, working at local, national and regional levels. At the local/national level, there are two main types of institutions: National Appropriate Technology Committees, set up by governments to advise on technology policy, promote and co-ordinate AT activities, and liaise with external AT institutions; and Appropriate Technology Development Centres, set up by governments, academic institutions, or non-governmental organizations to generate and implement appropriate technologies. At the regional level, there are also two main types of initiative: Regional Committees and Centres set up by member governments to promote the use of technologies appropriate to their needs and circumstances; and Regional Networks set up by non-governmental AT groups to promote the interchange of information, technologies, experience and expertise.

A. National Appropriate Technology Committees

In many countries, there are a large number of governmental and non-governmental agencies whose policies and activities directly or indirectly impinge on technology development and implementation: there are also many voluntary agencies concerned specifically with appropriate technology. Frequently, these agencies work in isolation from each other, and efforts may be duplicated or hindered by the actions of others. As governments have become more interested in the concept and application of AT, the need has been identified for some mechanism which can advise on technology policy in a broad sense, monitor and co-ordinate activities, and promote and act as a focus for new initiatives, so that AT can be more systematically implemented on a widespread basis.

In response to this need, governments in several countries have established a National Appropriate Technology Committee (NATC) as a co-ordinating institution which, in theory at least, has the power to influence significantly the direction of technology development and the rate at which appropriate technologies are effectively disseminated and used. Within Africa, NATCs have been established in Malawi, Zambia, Tanzania, Kenya and Sierra Leone, largely as a result of recommendations arising from rural technology meetings sponsored by the Commonwealth Secretariat's Food Production and Rural Development Division. Other countries, including the Seychelles, Zimbabwe, and the Gambia, are pursuing the establishment of NATCs.

In these countries, it is intended that the NATCs should be composed of representatives of relevant ministries and, as appropriate, respresentatives of technical institutions, parastatals, the banking and commercial sector, and voluntary agencies. In some cases (notably Malawi, where the NATC secretariat is located in the National Research Council), the NATC is composed of senior representatives of all the concerned agencies. In others (such as Sierra Leone, where the secretariat is in the University), representation is by junior officials. In others (such as Tanzania, where the secretariat is in the Ministry of Agriculture), there are important gaps in coverage (such as the exclusion in Tanzania of the parastatal concerned with small-scale industrial development).

The functions of the NATCs include: promotion and co-ordination of AT research and development; promotion of the planning and implementation of AT programmes; and liaison with AT Institutions outside the country to assist the effective transfer of technology. Only in the case of Malawi is the NATC charged with vetting foreign technology for appropriateness and with recommending AT policy as part of overall government policy.

Typically, the NATCs meet on a regular basis to discuss on-going activities in the field, identify gaps and bottlenecks, and make recommendations for action. Most NATCs have, or are planning to set up specialized sub-committees which draw on a wider range of expertise in each particular technical area.[6]

NATCs are only effective if they can translate their ideas and recommendations into action, which entails having a permanent secretariat with some executive power. This is the case in Malawi, where, moreover, the NATC's position in the government structure (in the National Research Council within the Office of the President and Cabinet) allows it to advise on policies and programmes in all sectors of the economy. None of the other NATCs have permanent secretariats with executive power, and consequently they have little power to do more than discuss issues and the need for action. Even with a permanent secretariat with executive power, the effectiveness of an NATC will greatly depend upon where they are located in the government structure.

While a NATC with the right membership and a well-located secretariat may be able to influence government policy and the programmes of existing research and extension agencies, it has no real capacity to supplement their resources so as to fill gaps in the implementation of AT programmes. This lack of an 'action arm' has been noted by even the Malawi NATC, which has recommended the establishment of a technology centre with personnel and financial resources: the scope and nature of such a centre and its relationship to the NATC and the secretariat remain to be worked out.

The Science and Technology Committee in Guyana is one of the few examples of NATCs outside of Africa. Its secretariat is within the National Science Research Council, through which it advises government on technology policy. Government support has been obtained to establish the Institute of Applied Science and Technology (IAST) as the action arm of the committee to implement AT projects in collaboration with existing agencies.

A somewhat different example is that of the Standing Committee for Appropriate Technology set up by the Indonesian government to improve co-ordination of AT activities. The Committee's Chairman was from the

Indonesian Institute of Science (LIPI), which has responsibility for advising government on science and technology policy. With advice and assistance from UNIDO/UNDP, an AT Unit was established in LIPI which would serve as the secretariat for the committee and would also be a focus for AT in the country by collecting and disseminating information, identifying gaps and advising the committee on action needed, and liaising with external agencies. However, this initiative has met with little enthusiasm from other agencies in Indonesia. This suggests that attempts to combine an NATC with an AT Centre may be more complicated than the process of simply establishing a committee (which can often be done with no more than the passive support of government and other relevant agencies).

B. Appropriate Technology Development Centres

Unlike NATCs, which are set up mainly to advise and co-ordinate, Appropriate Technology Development Centres (ATDCs) are set up mainly to generate and implement appropriate technologies. Some are set up by governments to provide a focus for AT activities in the country by collecting and disseminating information to relevant agencies, and by identifying gaps and bottlenecks and taking action to resolve them using existing agencies and facilities within (and if necessary from outside) the country. Others are set up by governments to serve more specific functions such as providing a technological input into training and extension schemes or demonstrating approaches to the application of AT on a pilot project basis.

Academic institutions and non-governmental organizations have also established ATDCs with much the same purposes in mind — usually at a local rather than national level. Some seek to gain recognition as a national focus for AT work, although few have managed to do so. Several, however, have had considerable success in gaining government support for expanding or replicating their activities.

1. Government-sponsored/controlled Appropriate Technology Development Centres

A number of governments have responded to the need for more systematic application of appropriate technology by establishing ATDCs or AT units attached to, or as an integral part of, government ministries, parastatals or research and development institutions: examples include Lesotho, Botswana, Papua New Guinea, Nepal, Tanzania and Colombia [7].

These ATDCs are expected by government to provide a focus for AT activities in the country. Their functions usually include: identifying major problem areas where development is inhibited by lack of appropriate technology; seeking out and analysing possible technological solutions to these problems; in the absence of immediate solutions, commissioning existing agencies to improve or adapt available technologies or develop new technologies; and assisting with the implementation of such technologies through organizing the production and testing of field prototypes, establishing pilot production plants or other services needed to supplement the resources of existing agencies.

An ATDC is usually responsible to a governing board that consists of representatives from relevant ministries, technical institutes, parastatals and voluntary agencies. Although the agencies represented on these boards are much the same as those which make up NATCs, there is an important difference: while the members of an NATC can only make recommendations for action, the members of an ATDC board can approve and authorize action and will automatically have some degree of executive power. The ATDC's effectiveness, however, will still largely depend on the composition of the board, and its status and location within the government structure.

Effectiveness will also depend on the capacity of its staff and its budget. ATDCs normally have specialist staff appointed from outside the government civil service, and are therefore less subject to bureaucratic constraints and other staff limitations associated with the civil service. When established as autonomous units, ATDCs have an independent budget normally made up of grants from the government and a variety of international donor agencies.

Recommendations to establish autonomous ATDCs to benefit from these advantages have not always been accepted, as exemplified in Lesotho. The original proposal to establish an ATDC recommended an autonomous unit,[8] but in the event the Lesotho AT Unit was established as an integral part of the parastatal responsible for small industry development, without any authority in the sectors outside the terms of reference of that parastatal (such as agriculture and energy). Thus the Lesotho AT Unit has been unable to be the focus for all AT activity, and the scope of its work has been severely limited. An attempt was made to broaden its influence by establishing an informal inter-ministerial committee, but this also lacked the power to authorize involvement in sectors other than small industry. Efforts to relocate and restructure the Lesotho AT Unit have continued as yet without result.

With this experience in mind, considerable time and effort was invested to ensure that the Botswana Technology Centre (BTC) was established as an autonomous ATDC with the support and resources required to fulfill its objectives.[9] Since BTC's main function was to identify gaps in research and development and extension, and to select and commission others to undertake the necessary work, rather than undertake the work itself, full support and co-operation from the relevant agencies was essential. Some of these agencies initially resented the creation of a new unit, either believing that they themselves could adequately provide the focus for AT, or fearing that the new unit would control rather than supplement their activities. Co-operation was obtained by involving such agencies throughout the establishment process, by giving them representation on the BTC Board, and by stressing the support for BTC of key government ministries (whose support was, in turn, needed by the other agencies).

Care was also taken in the selection of a director and other key staff,[10] and the acquisition of funds and establishment of a budget that allowed BTC to undertake a meaningful programme (particularly to commission work to be done by indigenous agencies). This establishment process required some three years of negotiation and another year of setting-up: while this delayed the start of actual work, the time and effect has proved worthwhile, as the BTC is now firmly established and operating effectively.

Another governmental ATDC is the South Pacific Appropriate Technology Foundation (SPATF) in Papua New Guinea. The Government's Office of Village Development established SPATF as an independent company with responsibility for the transfer of technology to the villages. SPATF has its own budget, considerable freedom of action, and a powerful governmental board.

With a rural extension affiliation and direction, SPATF concentrated initially on the software aspects of AT: methodologies for technology needs assessment were worked out, technical information from within and outside the country was collected and analysed to find appropriate technological solutions to rural problems, and training courses and other communications tools were developed to transfer these to the rural areas. The staff was backed up with technical advice from faculty of the University of Technology at Lae: SPATF later seconded staff and gave other support to establish the Appropriate Technology Development Institute (ATDI)[11] in conjunction with the University to develop the hardware side of its work.

The prototypes which arise from the more innovative research and development work of ATDI need considerable field testing under actual working conditions in rural communities to prove their technical feasibility and economic viability; and work is continuing on the development of a suitable methodology for this. For less complicated technologies, SPATF has established a workshop and testing area where ideas can be translated into prototypes and tested for feasibility in conditions similar to those found in many villages. To further facilitate dissemination of AT in rural areas, SPATF has also set up a trading arm, Village Equipment Suppliers (VES), which imports equipment that cannot yet be made locally and which is then sold at low prices in the rural areas (particularly to self-help projects). VES also provides advice on equipment choice, training in use and maintenance, and after-sales service. This is a unique AT marketing scheme which would appear to have relevance for other AT Institutions in other countries.

SPATF has recently moved into small-scale industrial development. It has two small industry schemes which provide direct employment and serve as models for possible replication. In one scheme, the businesses are owned by the workers who operate them, with SPATF providing central facilities and support services. In the other, the businesses are wholly owned by SPATF: this commercial venture has its own Board, at whose discretion profits are channelled back into SPATF to help support its non-profit activities.

Thus, SPATF has become an umbrella organization with a number of independent commercial and non-profit-making companies. This unique model warrants further investigation to determine whether it could be replicated elsewhere.

In Nepal, rather than starting from extension/rural development, the government has initially placed the focus for AT activities within the state-controlled scientific research and development network. In 1979, the Research Centre for Applied Science and Technology (RECAST) was established from an existing institute and charged with collecting information, identifying gaps and facilitating action to generate and disseminate appropriate technologies, and with undertaking technology development activities.[12] In addition, it was to provide the secretariat for the National Council for Science and Technology, which has responsibility for the formulation of science and technology policy and co-ordination of all scientific research.

With a background of scientific research and a staff largely of academically-oriented scientists, RECAST has made little headway in helping to solve the technological problems of farmers or industrial entrepreneurs. The staff are concentrated in the section dealing with research and development, while the extension section has no staff at all (the reason cited is the problem of finding and training technical people with suitable qualifications and skills). Secondly, the parastatals responsible for extending advice to small farmers and industry have not been involved with RECAST, which has not, therefore made any significant use of their experience and resources. RECAST's difficulty in working on such problems and its lack of capacity or interest in the field testing of prototypes or extension has been pointed out by the many agencies from which it has sought financial and technical assistance. This weakness is acknowledged by Government and attempts are underway to counteract it: for example, scientific staff are being given engineering training outside the country, an outreach centre has been established, and substantial funding has been sought to provide expatriate AT capacity to strengthen the extension section.

In Colombia, the government's National Training Service (SENA) set up a Technology Division to investigate technological needs (particularly in the rural areas), to seek out and develop solutions, and to bring about widespread application of the solutions through the training and extension activities of staff in the SENA regional offices. The Technology Division concentrated almost totally on laboratory research, and relied on staff in the regional offices to supply it with information on needs and to transfer the solutions it identified or developed. Problems were encountered in the determination of priority areas of need, and in the identification of constraints on production. There was too much emphasis on technical factors against economic/financial factors and a concentration on hardware to the neglect of software. There was also insufficient attention to the market. The Technology Division failed to meet its objectives using this approach, and has recently been disbanded.

Las Gaviotas in Columbia and the Arusha Appropriate Technology Project (AATP) in Tanzania are both government-sponsored pilot projects established to demonstrate the methodology for applying AT to assist rural communities, in the hope that successfully developed methodologies would be taken up by government and others for replication in other parts of the country. After many years of work, both projects have had a noticeable impact on their project areas.

In the process, however, they have absorbed a large amount of resources in relation to the number of rural people assisted Working out new models and methodologies can be expected to use up considerable resources, and cost-savings can usually be expected with widespread replication (analogous with the high cost of developing a prototype, and the lower costs that can be expected once it goes into commercial production). In the case of Las Gaviotas, international funding has been obtained to allow the pilot project to be repeated in another small are as an interim step to allow modifications before replication. In the AATP's case, the Tanzanian Government has questioned whether sufficient resources could be made available to replicate the methodology throughout the country, and has carried out an evaluation to identify less resource-intensive modifications.

Since a government ATDC is expected to become involved in the implementation of technologies, it needs both expert staff and an adequate budget. Typically this requires the use of expatriate personnel[14] The extent to which ATDCs use expatriate personnel is related to the funding received from donor agencies. Core and project support for government ATDCs has come from a variety of multilateral and bilateral donors, international NGOs and the national governments themselves. Only SPATF in Papua New Guinea appears, as yet, to have made any significant progress in earning its own income.

2. Academic/Research Institutes with Appropriate Technology Development Centres.

This category of ATDCs typically results from the initiative of small groups of engineering teachers who have felt that university faculty, students and facilities could do much more to help national development by generating technologies which promote self-reliance or are appropriate to the means and needs of small entrepreneurs and the rural poor. They include the Technology Consultancy Centre (TCC) at the University of Science and Technology, Kumasi, Ghana; the Advisory Services Unit for Technology Research and Development (ASTRAD) at Fourah Bay College, Sierra Leone; the Cell for Application of Science and Technology in Rural Areas (ASTRA) at the Indian Institute of Management, Bangalore, India; the Small Industry Research, Training and Development Organisation (SIRTDO) at the Birla Institute of Technology, Ranchi, India; the Development Technology Centre (DTC) at the Bandung Institute of Technology, Indonesia: the Appropriate Technology Development Institute (ATDI), at the University of Technology, Lae, Papua New Guinea; and numerous others.[15]

One way in which such an initiative is undertaken is by the establishment of a committee which acts as a catalyst in persuading faculty and students to work on AT, and identifies and secures funds for projects (as with ASTRAD and ASTRA). The other approach is to establish an autonomous ATDC within the University which has full-time staff and resources of its own, but also draws on the faculty, students and facilities of the University (as with TCC, SIRTDO, DTC and ATDI).

Institutionally it is considerably easier to establish a committee within an existing organization than to set up an autonomous unit. This approach also side steps the problem of finding core funding, and enables concerned individuals to work on AT projects on a part-time basis without giving up the security and prestige of their university appointment. However, reliance on voluntary effort and lack of full-time staff presents a severe limitation. ASTRAD's experience in Sierra Leone illustrates the problem. Having embarked with government on projects to develop and disseminate new technologies for rural use, the staff found that their teaching responsibilities required them to undertake new projects with students in the laboratories, which left inadequate time to get involved in the identification of needs, in producing commercial prototypes, or in field testing and prototype modification.

To some extent, ASTRA in India has resolved this problem by bringing about changes in teaching curricula that allow students to obtain a degree by working full-time on rural technology projects based in ASTRA's field station under the supervision of ASTRA faculty members. Although this methodology has received international recognition, there has yet been no significant application of technology and only a few faculty members provide more than occasional support for the work. By the late 1970s, ASTRA had recognized that further development of its work would require core support for the recruitment of full-time staff.

Obtaining core support for an autonomous ATDC is not easy: one useful approach appears to be to work with volunteer or part-time staff until the ideas proposed have been shown to be workable. Once established, the problem limiting development often is the difficulty in finding suitably qualified indigenous technical staff (rather than to secure funding). Accordingly, many such ATDCs (including TCC, ATDI and DTC) have made extensive use of expatriate engineers and volunteers. Others (such as SIRTDO) have acquired staff on secondment from an institute of applied scientific research.

Autonomous ATDCs within academic or research institutes have started off by concentrating either on technologies appropriate for small industries and entrepreneurs (TCC, SIRTDO) or on technologies appropriate for the needs of rural communities (DTC, ATDI). Experience indicates that they have had more success with the first category. Possibly, this is because it is much easier for a small group of university-based professionals to handle (or at least co-ordinate) the software elements involved in transferring technologies to urban and semi-urban small entrepreneurs than to widely-dispersed rural artisans amd communities. This does not imply that small industry development and promotion is a simple matter. The experience of TCC in Ghana and SIRTDO in Bihar show that it can take years of work with many setbacks before significant results are achieved. In both cases, the major problems were not so much in developing the technologies appropriate to small-scale production as with the commercialization of the products and processes once developed.

TCC found that small entrepreneurs were unwilling to invest in new processes in the absence of proof that they would form the basis of a profitable venture. The only way to overcome this was to set up and operate pilot production plants in the TCC workshops to demonstrate the technical and economic viability of the new processes. The commercial operation of these production units is a major undertaking, which requires much of the TCC staff's time. The production units do, however, provide income, accounting for nearly half of TTC's total income.

SIRTDO's approach has been somewhat different. Products needed by local heavy industry and capable of small-scale production were identified and laboratory models were developed by students and SIRTDO staff in the University's workshops. Industry, however, required commercial prototypes to test before giving any assurance of orders, but the University's workshops were not equipped (or allowed) to produce commercial prototypes. To resolve this, funds were obtained and technical personnel seconded from the Birla Institute of Scientific Research to set up and operate a workshop capable of developing commercial prototypes. Once markets were established, there was the problem of actual production, which was generally beyond the technical capabilities of existing small firms in the area. SIRTDO resolved this problem by helping some of the University graduates (many of whom had worked on developing the technologies as students) to set up small industries.[16]

TCC and SIRTDO have found that entrepreneurs require assistance in acquiring loans, installing equipment, and training a workforce, and also need technical support to overcome initial operational problems. SIRTDO's task is made more difficult in that its entrepreneurs are inexperienced. To help with this problem, SIRTDO has established a 'nursery' industrial estate adjacent to the campus. TCCs task is easier, in that it is largely dealing with established entrepreneurs; the entrepreneurs are widely dispersed, however, which has led TCC to establish satellite units in key informal industrial areas.

The transfer of technologies in rural areas is more difficult, and requires greater time and resources. Both TCC and SIRTDO cite lack of resources as an explanation of their relative lack of success in the dissemination of rural technologies. However, both have recently started new rural development initiatives, and have established autonomous units to handle their rural development work.

In some countries, such as Indonesia, university students are required to spend part of their time on practical work in rural areas. As involvement in rural problems is thus an acceptable part of university work, the environment would appear favourable for an ATDC generating and transferring technologies to rural communities. However, the experience of the Development Technology Centre of the Bandung Institute of Technology suggests that this is not sufficient. There appear to have been problems of inadequate interaction between hardware development and needs identification, insufficient effort on field testing prototypes, and an imbalance of staff and resources in favour of laboratory research work.

Similarly, university-based ATDCs in other countries have had little success in the generation and transfer of technologies to rural communities. In Papua New Guinea, evaluations of ATDI have cited problems of insufficient capacity to undertake more than a few pilot schemes, concentration on academically-oriented projects, and an inability of faculty and students to become adequately involved in rural development work.[17] An exception is the Universidad de Los Andes in Bogota, Columbia, which has developed an approach to apply its resources to rural development effectively. A formal agreement was established that allowed the staff and students of the Engineering Faculty to work in an integrated manner with the staff of a government-sponsored rural development programme at Las Gaviotas. A faculty member and a group of students move between the University and the rural development area, determining needs in the field, developing prototypes at the University, and testing the prototypes in the field: eventually, successful prototypes are produced in the rural development area. This approach resolves the problem of how to direct sufficient numbers of technically-qualified staff to work in the rural areas for a sufficient time.

These experiences suggest that successful development and transfer of technologies requires a well-planned methodology and input of substantial technological capacity over five years or more. Moreover, while technologies can be developed by small numbers of technologists within the university the transfer of technologies to rural areas requires many more people with a variety of non-technical skills, and requires the ATDCs to work through existing rural development programmes. The technologists must still spend substantial time in the rural areas, which they may be unable or unwilling to do. It is thus easier for university-based ATDCs to transfer technologies to small entrepreneurs, although this still requires a commitment by the staff to apply their skills for the benefit of others.

With the exception of the Indian Groups (which have relied on assistance from the industrial giants, Birla and Tata, which established their parent organizations), all of the university-based ATDCs have received substantial external funding and/or technical assistance from a variety of bilateral multilateral and NGO sources. All receive assistance in cash or in kind from their parent organizations and national/state governments. TCC and SIRTDO have also succeeded in generating income of their own.

Relationships with governments go beyond direct funding. Many ATDCs hope eventually to influence government action by their example, although few groups say so in their written objectives. A notable success in this respect is SIRTDO, which has so impressed the Bihar State Government that it has directed all government technical colleges in the state to set up similar schemes and has allocated funds to allow them to do so.

3. **NGO Appropriate Technology Development Centres.**
Typically, this category of ATDC has been started by a few highly-motivated in `:viduals, who, in the apparent absence of interest elsewhere, have set out to generate and disseminate technologies appropriate to the needs and means of small entrepreneurs and the rural poor. Such organisations would appear to have the odds strongly against them, but several have had considerable success and have built up sizeable organisations with good support: these include the Centro

de Estudios Mesoamericanos y de Technologia Apropida (CEMAT) in Guatemala, Dian Desa in Indonesia, and the Appropriate Technology Development Association (ATDA) in India.

Apparent keys to success include: concentration on a small number of technical areas which reflect the technical expertise of their senior staff and for which there is an effective rural demand; a decentralized approach that makes substantial use of rural-based staff; and an ability to commercialize products and processes by both demonstrating their economic and technical viability in the rural areas, and training local people in their construction, use, maintenance and repair.

CEMAT has concentrated on basic rural needs. Its work on domestic stoves exemplifies its approach. On the basis of tests carried out in the university and in a number of rural areas, a stove design was identified that offered major fuel wood savings. CEMAT staff (many of whom are part-time staff living in the same area where they work) then visited rural communities to discuss needs and to present technical alternatives. On the request of rural communities (and for a nominal payment), CEMAT then organized training courses in which prototype stoves were constructed and the course participants developed the expertise and confidence to build stoves for the rest of the community.[18]

Dian Desa has also concentrated on basic rural needs, and works in much the same way as CEMAT, except that greater use is made of university volunteers for project work, and communities do not contribute financially in the testing and demonstration stages. Recently, Dian Desa has turned to the development of technologies for small-scale industry, and has obtained funds to establish a large workshop and other facilities to carry out this work. This will require different technical and commercial skills and a different approach. It remains to be seen if Dian Desa will have significant difficulties in making these changes (as, for example, TCC and SIRTDO did in moving from small-scale industry to rural development).

Rather than working on rural development, ATDA in

India has concentrated on scaling-down technologies to permit small-scale decentralized production, and its approach is thus different. Particular technologies are studied to determine if small-scale production is possible. If so, a pilot project is undertaken to develop a production unit which is then tested in a rural area for technical feasibility, economic viability, and commercial applicability. If successful, a turnkey package is then made available to prospective entrepreneurs. ATDA remains alongside the entrepreneurs during initial operations to assist in the resolution of technical problems. Although the development of a particular technology through this approach may take many years, ATDA believes that its method is necessary in order to win the confidence and support of decision-makers and users.[19]

Many other NGO ATDCs have been established,[20] but most have had little success in implementing AT projects. Reasons for this may include mismatches between the technical expertise of the staff and the needs of the areas under consideration, insufficient care in developing a methodology for identifying technologies for which there is effective demand, and inability to transfer technologies to potential users. These problems are in part exemplified in the Small Farm Equipment Unit of the Tikonko Agricultural Extension Centre in Sierra Leone, and the Society for Research and Application of Technology (SRAT) in Upper Volta. The Small Farm Equipment Unit was set up to develop mechanized equipment for the Centre's swamp rice development programme. Since many of the products developed were too expensive for all but the wealthiest farmers, there was little effective demand for them, and, in the absence of such demand, local entrepreneurs were uninterested in starting production. The Unit is now concentrating on producing cheaper items, which are selling well, though raw materials shortages, have restricted the Unit's production and have prevented the transfer of production to local entrepreneurs.

SRAT was established with support from two international NGOs to develop AT hardware. Various prototypes were designed and tested, but funds were inadequate to prove economic and technical viability, and government training and extension agencies and local entrepreneurs would not commit themselves to significant production without such proof. SRAT has obtained further funding for an experimental production unit to help overcome this problem, but dissemination remains limited.

Without government or university support, funding is an important issue for NGO ATDCs, particularly during their initial development. Nascent organizations are inevitably caught in a chicken and egg problem of needing a 'track record' of accomplishment to attract donors while having limited funds with which to develop such a record. Donor agencies have a noticeable tendency to reject 'first time callers' regardless of their potential; it would appear critically important for donor agencies to develop a better methodology for investigating such first time callers, so that potential successes can be better identified.

All of the NGO ATDCs considered rely heavily on international NGOs and bilateral and multilateral aid agencies for both core and project support. ATDA, however, has obtained direct financial support from government for some of its projects, while Dian Desa, Tikonko and CEMAT have started to earn income through the sale of products and/or consultancy work.[21] Personnel is also a major issue, as the quantity and quality of staff appears to determine progress as much as the availability of funds. ATDA, Dian Desa and CEMAT were staffed at first by highly-qualified founding members. In such cases, the task has been to recruit enough additional experienced staff or to recruit and train younger staff so that reliance on the founder members is reduced: only CEMAT appears to have succeeded in this. Tikonko and SRAT were staffed initially by expatriates (mainly volunteers) and inexperienced local counterparts. Here, the task has been to train the counterparts to a level that allows the replacement of expatriate staff: neither group has accomplished this.

The question of relationships with the national government is also important. Although passive government support is sufficient when the activities of a NGO are carried out on a small scale, more positive support is needed if they are to have a wide impact. Both ATDA in India and Dian Desa in Indonesia have obtained substantial government support that has allowed significant expansion of their activities.[22] As yet, the other NGO ATDCs have had little success in gaining active government support.

C. Regional Institutions and Initiatives

1. Government-level Institutions and Initiatives

The Regional Centre for Technology Transfer (RCTT) was established by the United Nations ESCAP in Bangalore India in 1977 as a result of a resolution passed at UNCTAD IV in 1976 which called on the UN to set up transfer of technology centres in each of its regions. A similar centre, the African Regional Centre for Technology (ARCT) was established by ECA in Dakar, Senegal in 1979. The objectives of the centres include: setting up of a clearing house for intra-regional and inter-regional exchange of information and experience relating to technology development, adaptation and transfer; promoting the establishment of national centres and strengthening their capabilities in respect of technology development, adaptation and transfer; promoting interest in the concept of appropriate technology among government policymakers, administrators, industrialists and universities; promoting and organizing regional cooperation in research and development of technologies appropriate to several countries in the region; improving, for the benefit of its member states, the terms and conditions under which technology is imported; and promoting within its member states the formulation of policies and planning concerning technology as an integral part of national socio-economic development.

Although the centres refer to appropriate technology (in the sense of technology appropriate to small entrepreneurs and the rural poor) in their objectives, their orientation is more towards developing regional and national technological capacity as a whole, to reducing dependence of member states on imported technologies, and on obtaining more favourable terms for member states on trasferred technologies.

As yet, RCTT seems to have concentrated on developing its information networking function, including the sponsoring of regional meetings on documentation information systems, and preparing and disseminating a technical digest. ARCTs initial work includes the collection and documentation of information on technology centres and on technologies developed or in use in Africa. While it is too early to assess the work of these centres, they are potentially in a strong position to influence technology policies, institutional developments, and technology programmes and projects, at both the regional and national levels. Moreover, they could encourage the kind of political, social and economic environment in member countries that would support the efforts of the various national and local AT institutions.

The initiatives that have been taken at the UN/government level to establish regional mechanisms have been essentially concerned with technology transfer and very few have been specifically concerned with appropriate technology. One initiative concerned with AT was the Technology Relay, started by the Environment Development Training Programme (ENDA), a UN-affiliated agency located in Dakar, Senegal. Its objectives were to collect and disseminate AT information within West Africa, answer technical enquiries through referral to regional experts, conduct research on indigenous technologies and disseminate the findings, conduct training workshops, and offer consultancy services. Such programmes require the involvement of other agencies, and, unless funds are available to allow these agencies to take on the extra staff to handle the additional work, there is likely to be a limited response. The Technology Relay had insufficient personnel and funds and could not commission work to be done by other agencies. Within two years, the Technology Relay was dormant.

A further government-level regional AT initiative is the Commonwealth Secretariat Food Production and Rural Development Division's programme to encourage the formation of Regional AT Committees (RATCs). The members of the RATCs are representatives of the NATCs and other national-level focal points within the region. The RATCs' functions are, in part, similar to those of the UN Centres, including information services, co-ordination of regional research and development, and the encouragement of national-level AT Institutions. Although it is a more appealing approach to start with the national-level institutions and get them to build up their own regional mechanism — rather than creating a regional centre which then has to establish links with existing national institutions — little headway has been made in forming these Regional Committees. The Commonwealth Secretariat maintains that this is because the NATCs first want to get properly established and their programmes underway. Alternatively national governments may see no need for a further regional initiative where a UN Regional Technology Centre already exists.

2. Non-governmental Institutions and Initiatives.

While the approach of building up regional networks from and for national AT institutions has, as yet, met with little success at the governmental level, it has had more success at the non-governmental level. A number of non-governmental regional networks has been formed, essentially to promote the exchange of information and experience. They differ, however, in structure and orientation.

Fourteen organizations in eleven Asian countries (with support from the International Development Research Centre, Canada) established Technonet as an exchange centre for information on technologies suitable for small/medium-scale industries, to be used mainly to train industrial extension staff. Currently, the network is being expanded in scope and size (with support from AT International, USA) to become the Asian Alliance of Appropriate Technology Practitioners (AAATP), with the existing Technonet Secretariat in Singapore becoming the temporary secretariat for AAATP. The objectives of the expanded network are to promote the exchange of technology and expertise by providing information, evaluation, screening and dissemination services to its members, and to serve as a bridge to decrease their isolation from activities elsewhere in the world.

In 1977, Christian Action for Development in the Caribbean (CADEC) established its Appropriate Technology Referral Service as an information exchange centre to serve the entire Caribbean. Lack of funds and personnel, however, resulted in it becoming largely a documentation centre/ technical enquiry service for CADEC's programme staff. In 1981 it was decided at a regional workshop attended by representatives from throughout the Caribbean that a truly regional information clearing house was needed. It was decided that NATCs should be established in each territory to undertake the development and promotion of AT, with a Caribbean AT Centre established at CADECs headquarters (in Barbados) providing information and other necessary support services to the NATCs. The value of the new centre will depend upon the success of the NATCs, which in turn will require specific advice on institutional development as well as funds.

In Latin America, the Comité de Coordinación y Promoción de Technología Apropiada (COCOP) was also established to promote the exchange of information and experience between national-level NGOs. COCOP has the unique characteristic of having no central secretariat.. The secretariat function revolves on an annual basis between the collaborating groups, with funds sought by the COCOP Committee to allow each group to take on the information function. The networking system in Latin America appears to be very well developed; it also has the distinction of being indigenously conceived and controlled. As such, it merits further investigation to determine its potential for replication elsewhere.

D. Summary

Initiatives have been taken at both national/local and regional levels, and at both government and non-government levels, to establish committees to promote the concept of appropriate technology and to coordinate AT activities, and to establish centres to generate and implement AT. In addition, initiatives have been taken at the regional level to set up networking systems primarily to strengthen national institutions through the exchange of information and experience.

At the national level, governments have only become directly involved in AT since the mid-1970s, and most of the NATCs and ATDCs they have established have not reached maturity. Nonetheless, their experiences are informative. First, it is easier to set up an NATC than an ATDC, since the former requires no special commitment of staff or funds and only passive support for AT from the government and other agencies in the country. However, an NATC will be able to accomplish little unless it has a powerful secretariat, and, if it is to have significant influence on government policy, the secretariat must be located in a key position within the government structure. Even then the NATC will have difficulty in translating its ideas into action without an 'action arm', which will require staff, funds and active support.

National ATDCs are expected by government to be actively involved in the implementation of AT projects, and their establishment, complete with a staff and budget of their own, indicates a real commitment by the government to AT. The ways and means by which they work, the problems they encounter, and their effectiveness in meeting their objectives depend on a variety of factors, including their institional affiliation (that is, whether they are linked to a parastatal, an extension ministry, a planning ministry, or a research and development institute), their organizational structure (whether they are independent organizations or totally-controlled units of a ministry or parastatal), and the size and skills of their staff. Although some ATDCs may advise government on specific AT projects, they normally have no brief to vet the technology component of other development projects or to advise on changes in policy to bring about a more favourable environment for AT.

University groups and non-governmental organizations have concentrated on proving the viability of AT through demonstration in localized areas. Their main objective has been to show the application of AT can contribute to national development, in order to obtain government (and other) support to replicate their activities on a more widespread basis. Many such ATDCs have been operating for five to ten years, and are considerably more mature than governmental AT institutions.

University groups have tended to concentrate on research and development rather than extension. They have had considerable success in developing and transferring new technologies to small (usually urban) entrepreneurs, and government support has been obtained by some ATDCs for the expansion of activities or replication. They have been less successful in developing and transferring technologies to rural communities, mainly because of the lack of resources and skilled staff who can spend the required time in rural areas.

On the other hand, non-governmental organizations that concentrate on a few technical subject areas in which their staff have specific expertise have often worked successfully on rural technology programmes, both in establishing small rural industries and in improving living standards in rural communities. Without institutional affiliation they have had to develop a methodology for utilising the research and development facilities and extension services of others, and some have become skillful at this, thus allowing concentration of their own resources on neglected aspects of the implementation process.

Many university and NGO ATDCs have not been successful, either because they have failed to recognise some of the steps in the complex process of developing and transferring technologies, or because they have as yet failed to identify effective ways of handling the steps.

Apart from, but related to, the difficulties in developing a successful methodology, the University and NGO groups have encountered other common problems. These include attracting core and project funding for their work, recruiting experienced staff, and gaining acceptance for their ideas and methodology from government and others. Attracting funding appears to be the least of these problems (once a 'track record' has been established), although there is a trend towards generating income to reduce external financial dependence. The other two problems have yet to be successfully resolved, except in isolated cases.

A considerable merging effect is observable in the experiences of all national/local level AT institutions — whether initiated by govenments, universities or NGOs. NATCs have tended to move towards the establishment of centres, while the ATDCs have often seen the need to take on some of the advisory and co-ordinating functions characteristic of the committees. Research and development institutions have been moving into extension and training while extension and training agencies have been moving to increase the technological input in their work. This is only to be expected, sine the development and dissemination of appropriate technologies is a complex process, and the institutions involved are constantly being made aware of their limitations in dealing with it. To overcome their limitations, they have started new initiatives of their own and/or sought the assistance of other institutions. How this moulding and meshing process is being done or could be done is far from clear: further institutional research and development work is needed if advice is to be given with any degree of confidence.

Most regional initiatives have been taken within the last five years, and there is not yet sufficient information and experience to assess them. However, the regional centres established through the United Nations have no specific interest in appropriate technology, and are unlikely to pay significant attention to it without pressure being brought to bear by member governments (through for example, the advice of NATCs). Non-governmental regional initiatives have mainly aimed at strengthening links between member groups through the exchange of information and experience. When developed and controlled by the member groups, this approach must have potential for strengthening the programme of the groups, but it is not yet clear exactly how this could be best done.

III. APPROPRIATE TECHNOLOGY INSTITUTIONS IN DEVELOPED COUNTRIES

A large proportion of the AT institutions located in developed countries are in the USA, and are involved in the generation and implementation of appropriate technology in their own country; these are outside the concern of this review. However, some of the developed country institutions focus their attention on the technical needs of poorer sectors of developing countries. They work in different ways and face different problems to AT institutions located in developing countries; in essence, the former have to find ways of working through and providing effective support to the latter and to other relevant agencies in the developing countries.

AT institutions in developed countries fall into three major categories: those established or supported by their governments; those attached to an academic/research institute; and non-governmental organizations. In addition, there are a number of governmental and non-governmental agencies in the developed countries which, although they have no specific units or programmes aimed at providing technical assistance or advice to AT institutions in developing countries, have contributed substantial financial and other support, either directly or through specialised AT institutions in their own country.

A. Government-sponsored/controlled Institutions

Governments in developed countries have shown an increasing interest in the concept of appropriate technology. Some, such as the governments of the USA, UK, Germany, France, and the Netherlands, have supported the establishment of national autonomous AT institutions and/or have channelled funds for appropriate technology programmes overseas through existing AT institutions in their own country.

In the USA, Appropriate Technology International (ATI) was created in 1977 as an independent, non-profit institution. This was in response to a Congressional mandate for a co-ordinated private effort to promote the development and dissemination of AT in developing countries, and a subsequent USAID proposal to Congress to establish a private organization to help developing countries to strengthen their capacities to develop, adapt and utilize appropriate technologies. ATI administers a fund of US$ 20 million. It has used this mainly to strengthen local delivery systems (including AT institutions) in developing countries to increase access of the poor to the technologies needed to sustain their own development. It also assists small enterprises and community groups to undertake productive ventures with a potential for commercialization. ATI does not engage in projects itself, and offers logistic rather than technical support to overseas institutions.

USAID has become involved in other major AT programmes in developing countries. As part of this initiative, it has allocated US$ 10 million to Volunteers in Technical Assistance (VITA) to strengthen the NGO's capacity to undertake renewable energy projects, and has directly supported major renewable energy projects in several countries.[22]

In the UK, Intermediate Technology Industrial Services (ITIS) was set up in 1978 following a Ministry of Overseas Development Working Party which recommended that aid activities to advance AT should be intensified. ITIS, although totally supported by the Overseas Development Administration (ODA), is an integral part of the Intermediate Technology Development Group (ITDG). It aims at meeting the needs of developing countries for unfamiliar or new technologies in the small industry sector through dissemination of information, answering of technical enquiries, and financial and technical assistance for prototype development and testing and for market analyses. It has had considerable success in working with AT institutions and private entrepreneurs in developing countries in bringing such technologies to implementation. As part of the same initiative, ODA has allocated funds to allow ITDG to set up an AT Institutions Unit and to set aside a small technical assistance fund for the benefit of AT institutions in developing countries.

ODA also totally supports the Tropical Products Unit (TPI). TPI's overall function is to assist developing countries by considering the scientific, technical and economic problems which arise after harvesting. Its Industrial Development Department has undertaken research and development on technologies appropriate to post-harvest needs in developing countries and has established collaborative programmes with institutions (mainly government departments or government-sponsored agencies) in these countries. In addition, ODA has allocated funds for specific research and development projects, particularly in the field of energy, to be carried out in conjunction with overseas institutions. Some of these funds have been channelled through ITDG/ITIS.

In Germany, the German Appropriate Technology Exchange (GATE) was created in 1978 as a small section within GTZ, the Federal Government's aid executing agency. It is wholly supported by the Ministry of Economic Cooperation and the Ministry for Research and Technology. GATE has a technical enquiry and information service, and identifies and formulates collaborative technology programmes in developing countries, particularly in renewable energy. It also has a mandate for evaluating the projects of German research and development institutions to ascertain whether products and processes developed for the domestic market have any value for, and market in, developing countries. It has minor project funds for surveys of traditional technologies, publications, strengthening of information systems in developing country institutions, and for investigation of the potential for software exchange between German software institutions and national productivity centres, small business centres and the like in developing countries.

Most of GATE's staff are involved in information,

technical enquiries and publications work. A small number of core staff handle the identification and formulation of collaborative technology programmes (with considerable use of German consultants). The execution of programmes is passed to GTZ, although GATE (through consultants) may be involved in implementation if there is a need for on-going research and development.

In France, the Groupe de Recherche et Échange Technologique (GRET) was set up in 1975 by the Technical Cooperation Department of the Ministry of Foreign Affairs as an independent non-profit organization. Its purpose was mainly to collect and document information so as to answer technical enquiries from French development staff and volunteers in developing countries, and to train and orient French volunteers before they began to work overseas.

GRET has built up a large information centre, and publishes and disseminates considerable literature in French. Given the few AT institutions which can respond to requests for information in French, GRET plays a very important role in helping to fill information gaps in francophone countries. However, a recent government-commissioned evaluation of GRET's activities recommended that future funding should be dependent upon GRET's ability to become involved in collaborative projects with organizations in developing countries. Investigations are underway to ascertain how this information-oriented organization could so diversify.

In the Netherlands, the TOOL Foundation provides the focal point for government activity in appropriate technology for developing countries. TOOL was founded by a number of groups connected with various Dutch universities to coordinate their activities in response to technical enquiries from developing countries. It is a non-profit organization sponsored by the Netherlands Ministry of Development, and with some (but increasingly less) financial support from the collaborating universities.

Although TOOL has been involved in a few collaborative research and development projects with AT institutions in developing countries, most effort has been directed to responding to technical enquiries by referral to specialists in its member groups and through its documentation centre. As part of its information and documentation activites, TOOL was instrumntal in the establishment of the Socially Appropriate Technology Information Service (SATIS) which aims at enabling AT groups in both developing and developed countries to systemize and increase their capacity to respond to technical enquiries by being able to call on the work of other groups. The system involves each participating group classifying its information on technologies, recording details of each on fiches, and sending copies of these to the SATIS secretariat (within TOOL) which on request makes them available to affiliated groups. The original membership of SATIS was largely of groups in developed countries, but an increasing number of AT institutions in developing countries are using its classification system, without going into the more costly and time-consuming process of transcribing information on fiches and transmitting these to the secretariat.[23]

A recent government-commissioned evaluation of TOOL's activities recommended a reduction in the support given to the information and documentation side of the organization (including SATIS), and a greater concentration on project work in collaboration with overseas institutions.[24] Ways and means of strengthening the project side of the organization are now under investigation. At the same time, SATIS has sought increased contributions from its other members and from international funding agencies. There are also plans to move the SATIS secretariat from TOOL, perhaps to an agency in a developing country.

Besides its support for TOOL and the projects of TOOL's member groups, the Dutch Goverment has other funds for the promotion of appropriate technology which are channelled through foreign AT isntitutions or directly to AT institutions in developing countries.

Thus, in general, developed country AT institutions set up or wholly sponsored by their governments have — or are being directed towards — a project-oriented approach which involves collaborative work programmes with institutions in developing countries.[25]

B. Academic/Research Institutes with Appropriate Technology Units

Although there is increasing interest in appropriate technology in the science and engineering divisions of many universities in the developed countries, very few have specialized units which concentrate on research and development work related to the needs and circumstances of developing countries. Those with an interest in the technology problems of developing countries have focused on the establishment of courses in appropriate technology to broaden the context in which engineering and science are considered and to produce engineers and technologists with skills more appropriate to the needs and circumstances of developing countries.[26] This is an important role for such unversities, given that many of the students at universities in developed countries come from and return to the developing countries.

The few universities with AT units involved in collaborative projects with institutions in developing countries include the University of Delft in the Netherlands, and McGill University in Canada.[27] The Appropriate Technology Department at Eindhoven and the Centre for Appropriate Technology (CAT) at Delft were established through the voluntary efforts of a group of faculty members interested in technological problems in the Third World: the Brace Research Institute at McGill was set up as the result of a bequest to conduct research into methods of irrigation for desert or arid land and into renewable energy technologies.

The Dutch university-based AT units atarted by stimulating interest in AT within their universities and co-ordinating research in response to technical enquiries from Dutch volunteers and groups overseas. Although useful to faculty and students, it was seen that this approach had a limited potential for impact in developing countries, and that it was necessary to identify and formulate projects which could be implemented through collaborating organizations in the developing countries. Major projects were identified through the analysis of technical enquiries, but identification of counterpart organizations has proved more difficult. Overseas projects have been largely in countries with which the Netherlands has strong historical links (such as Indonesia and Sri Lanka), and have been funded by the Dutch Government. As yet, performance has been disappointing. Following a recent government evaluation of the AT programmes it supports, ways are being sought through which the university-based AT units could become more effectively involved in collaborative projects: these may be through TOOL, of which both AT units are members.

Over twenty years of operation, the Brace Research Institute has built up considerable capacity to offer advice and assistance in renewable energy technologies. Recognizing the importance of indigenous capacity, it has developed a policy of assisting the formation and strengthening of similarly-oriented institutions overseas through providing policy advice to governments, sharing of knowledge, and specialized training of staff from developing country institutions. Collaborative projects have also been undertaken with institutions in several countries.

C. Non-governmental Appropriate Technology Institutions

Specialized non-governmental AT institutions located in the developed countries include some of the first established and best known organizations in the AT movement, such as the Intermediate Technology Development Group (ITDG) in the UK, and Volunteers in Technical Assistance (VITA) in the USA. A basic concern of these organizations, and one which they were originally set up to address, was that appropriate technologies were often not selected and applied in developing countries because of lack of information about the hardware involved. Both ITDG and VITA began in a small way in the 1960s with voluntary contributions from small groups of technical people, and, as the demand for information and advice grew, both groups formed small non-profit organizations which gradually grew to their present size. Collecting and documenting information has been an important function of both groups, although they have adopted different approaches to the increasing and changing needs of the AT movement.

VITA was able to respond to the increasing number of technical enquiries by building up a large documentation centre and an associated classification and retrieval system. A roster of 'volunteers' was built up, both within and outside the USA, to give additional attention to specific technical enquiries: as enquiries became more difficult, volunteers who were 'on-the-spot' were used to help interpret responses. VITA also set about building up national capacities to respond to technical enquiries by encouraging the establishment of national groups in its image: five 'national VITAs' were established in Latin America in the early 1970s to document information of local relevance and to use national 'volunteers' to help with the technical enquiry service. VITA has also trained library staff and provided documentalists for AT institutions overseas.[28] Recently, VITA has appointed technical project officers (particularly in stoves and renewable energy technologies) to provide better assistance to AT institutions in developing countries through working on joint projects.

ITDG was able to respond to the increasing number of technical enquiries by working on a 'knowledge of knowledge' basis, whereby core staff refer all but the most general enquiries to the members of its technical panels, its technical project officers, and its subsidiary units. ITDGs technical panels are made up of experts from academic institutions, private industry and government, who give their assistance on a voluntary basis. The specialist technical project officers work on projects with overseas institutions and provide in-depth responses to technical enquiries. In some areas, such as energy and transport, ITDG has supported its project officers in establishing independent subsidiary companies under the umbrella of the parent group. Where enquiries are outside ITDG's area of current expertise, they are referred to specialist research institutions with which contacts have been developed. ITDG has never seen the need to centralize and systematize all its information, a source of puzzlement to those who ask to examine its documentation or information system.

ITDG has also increasingly referred technical enquiries to AT institutions located in developing countries (where enquiries originate). It has been involved in the establishment of many AT institutions[29] which have the capacity to respond to technical enquiries: however, in the belief that documentation/information is only one of the functions of such institutions, ITDG has also encouraged their research and development, and their extension capacity (particularly through joint technical projects).

In the 1970s, several other non-governmental AT groups were established in developed countries. These include the Appropriate Health Resources and Technology Action Group (AHRTAG) in the UK, the Association for Appropriate Technology in Developing Countries (ATOL) and the Collectif d'Echanges pour la Technologie Appropriée (COTA) in Belgium, and the Swiss Centre for Appropriate Technology (SKAT) in Switzerland. All have a strong information/documentation bias and regard responding to technical enquiries as their major function.

AHRTAG developed out of ITDG's Health Panel, and receives funding from WHO, SIDA and other agencies. Its primary function is seen as responding to technical enquiries in the area of low-cost health, through its documentation centre backed up by referral to experts and agencies with which it has developed contacts. Although starting primarily as an information service, it has identified knowledge gaps through analysis of enquiries, and now produces publications and undertakes hardware projects in collaboration with other agencies to fill such gaps. In particular, AHRTAG collaborates with ITDG/ITIS on hardware development and the production of health-related products in developing countries.

ATOL was established by returned volunteers, and COTA by a number of Belgian NGOs, to respond to technical enquiries from overseas volunteers and Belgian groups working in developing countries. Both also undertake the training of volunteers on behalf of the government, and seek to provide logistic support to overseas AT institutions. They have little core support, with most of their staff provided through governmental job-creation schemes. Both have converted to SATIS to improve their technical enquiry service. However, both have come to the conclusion that they must develop a capacity to undertake projects with overseas institutions: ways and means of doing this are being investigated, and a proposal has been submitted to the Government for funds to recruit technical project officers.

SKAT is supported by a variety of Swiss agencies. It also has realized the limitations of relying on the information documentation centre approach: difficulties have been experienced in providing sufficiently assessed responses to the increasing number of enquiries, particularly the more complicated enquiries from the more mature overseas AT institutions. SKAT is not currently planning to become directly involved in project work, but its staff do spend of their time overseas on consultancies to follow-up and consultants are used occasionally to give direct technical assistance to overseas groups. SKAT is also interested in assisting overseas AT institutions to respond to technical enquiries.

D. Other Initiatives of Government and Non-Governmental Organizations

Although they have no special appropriate technology units of their own, there are many governmental and non-governmental organizations in developed countries which have given considerable financial and logistic support to AT institutions in developing countries. Governmental initiatives include those of the Swedish aid agency (which has supported ENDA in Senegal and AATP in Tanzania), the New Zealand aid agency (support to SPATF in Papua New Guinea), the Canadian aid agency (support to IAST in Guyana), and the Canadian parastatal IDRC (support to CEMAT in Guatemala, and Technonet).

International NGOs that have given significant financial support to AT institutions in developing countries include OXFAM UK (which has supported SRAT in Upper Volta, Dian Desa in Indonesia and AATP in Tanzania), British

Christian Aid (support to ATDA in India), NOVIB and ICCO in the Netherlands (support to CEMAT in Gautemala and ATDA in India), Friedrich Neumann Foundation in Germany (support to Dian Desa in Indonesia), Bread for the World in Germany (support to CEMAT in Guatemala and ATDA in India), Rockefeller Foundation in the USA (support to TCC in Ghana), and the Canadian Freedom from Hunger Foundation (support to SPATF in Papua New Guinea).

Also worthy of mention are the various overseas volunteer schemes in the developed countries which have provided engineers and documentalists for AT institutions in developing countries. For example, Tikonko in Sierra Leone has had British (VSO), American (Peace Corps) and Canadian (CUSO) volunteers; Dian Desa in Indonesia has been assisted by the American-based Volunteers in Asia (VIA); and ATDI/Liklik Buk Centre in Papua New Guinea has benefited from British volunteers and staff seconded through the American branch of International Voluntary Service (IVS).

This varied source of funds and personnel has undoubtedly proved of value to the AT institutions in developing countries. Small NGO groups have particularly benefited from the provision of core support from international NGOs and have made use of the services of volunteers. Experience suggests, however, that although financial support is necessary, it is not sufficient to ensure the efficient working of an AT Centre. Similarly, volunteers have not always been able to provide skills of the required level, and often stay for insufficient time to bring a project to fruition or to train counterparts who can continue the work.

E. Summary

AT institutions in developed countries, whether they are initiated or supported by governments, universities or non-governmental organizations, can only have a significant impact on the process of developing and disseminating technologies appropriate to the needs and circumstancs of developing countries if they can find an effective way of working with, through or for institutions in these countries.

Initially, the task was that of making available general information on appropriate technology hardware, answering technical enquiries, and encouraging the establishment of AT institutions in developing countries. As the AT movement has grown, and as the AT institutions in developing countries have increased in number and maturity, the services which they require from AT institutions in the developed countries have changed. The need is now less for general information and answers to simple technical enquiries (although this is still of value) and more for specific in-depth technical assistance along with advice of an institutional or other non-technical nature.

AT institutions in developed countries have increasingly realized that it is necessary for them to find ways of becoming involved in project work in collaboration with overseas institutions, and to respond to requests for information and assistance on institutional and other non-technical problems. The various types of AT institution have approached these questions differently.

Government sponsored/controlled institutions have tended to concentrate on transferring information on commercial technologies available in their own countries, and increasingly, on working on ways and means of proving technical feasibility and economic viability in order to take technologies to widespread commercial application. Academic/research institutions have concentrated on providing more appropriate training for engineers and technologiests, rather than becoming too involved in collaborative projects overseas. Non-governmental institutions have tended to move away from documentation/information centres and networks and answering technical enquiries, and towards involvement in collaborative projects; with a few exceptions, the exact mechanisms by which this can be effectively done remain uncertain. While some of the specialist AT groups and many of the non-specialised funding agencies can provide financial and logistic support to overseas institutions, very few have any capacity to offer institutional advice with any degree of confidence.

IV. INTERNATIONAL INSTITUTIONS' INITIATIVES IN APPROPRIATE TECHNOLOGY

In the last few years, the United Nations and its various specialized agencies have become increasingly involved in appropriate technology. They work, of course, mainly through and with member governments, and their approach in most cases is a broad one — emphasizing appropriate choices of technolgoies and appropriate government policies overall — rather than the more specific approach of establishing or strengthening institutions concerned with technologies appropriate to the needs and circumstances of the rural and urban poor. There have, however, been a number of initiatives of the latter kind, and an attempt is made in this section to review these.

Also reviewed in this section are the experiences of the Commonwealth Secretariat in encouraging the establishment of AT committees at national and regional levels, and the work of the Transnational Network for Appropriate Technology (TRANET) which illustrates the experience of a non-governmental AT initiative at the international level.

A. International Labour Organisation (ILO)

ILO has incorporated appropriate technology in its work programme since the early 1970s, and in recent years has concentrated on the various constraints on the choice and application of more appropriate technologies as they relate to ensuring the satisfaction of basic needs. At a general level, ILO has commissioned several studies aimed at identifying institutional obstacles to the supply and demand for appropriate technologies in developing countries, and at identifying ways in which the policies, procedures and practices of governments in developed and developing countries affect technological decisions.

At a more specific level, ILO has supported the programmes of several regional and national technology centres, particularly in the dissemination of information on appropriate technology. For example, ILO co-sponsored (with ESCAP-RCTT) an Asian regional meeting to examine the documentation and information needs, facilities and systems which aid the choice of AT in the region: it has also organized study tours in the African region to allow representatives of national-level AT institutions to exchange experiences.

ILO has also been involved in attempts to establish an AT organization at the international level. In 1976, the ILO World Employment Conference proposed the establishment of an International AT Unit to provide a means of coordinating and disseminating AT work on a world-wide basis and to foster, encourage and disseminate research and development to meet the basic needs strategy. The International AT Unit would not undertake research and development itself, but would assist (by identifying gaps and helping to raise funds) national institutions (in developing countries where possible) to do so. Nor would it duplicate the information services of other institutions, but would catalogue who knows what and where and provide a link between national (and other international) institutions where necessary. This recommendation was later revived, in more or less the same form, with Dutch Government support, as a proposal for an International Mechanism for Appropriate Technology (IMAT). This proposal was based on the premise that existing initiatives of developed country and international agencies were inadequate. Not surprisingly, it has met with little support from such agencies: most such agencies accept that their initiatives have, as yet, had limited impact, but question the validity of trying to solve the problems by creating a new organization. A major reservation is that although the new organization is intended to be supportive and catalytic, it would duplicate activities of the existing agencies and divert funds away from their own proposed programmes for overcoming their current inadequacies.

At the level of national local AT Institutions, ILO has undertaken a technical assistance programme to promote the establishment of Rural Technology Centres linked to National Technology Centres. The proposed activities of the RTCs include: identifying needs and resources in their area of location; developing technologies to meet local needs and circumstances; initiating pilot projects to prove the technical feasibility and economic viability of new technologies; and organizing the production and use of such technologies through the provision of training and technical assistance to local entrepreneurs, astisans and communities. National Technology Centres (assumed by the ILO to be in existance) would disseminate technical information to the RTCs, train their staff, carry out laboratory testing of their designs, and co-ordinate, monitor and seek funding for their activities. Two programmes have been undertaken, with five RTCs established in Ecuador and three in Madagascar. Further programmes are expected to be funded by national governments and other interested agencies. Althouth this approach has considerable attractions, it raises serious questions with regard to the establishment of the RTCs, establishment of the NTC where one does not exist, relationships between the RTCs and NTC, and staffing a large rural programme.

B. United Nations Industrial Development Organisation (UNIDO)

In recent years, UNIDO has sought to assist developing countries in establishing adequate institutional frameworks for the development and dissemination of appropriate industrial technologies. It has worked at the country level through support for the creation of research and development institutions, technological information centres, and institutions for design, consultancy and engineering work. It has also worked at the international level through the organization of international exchanges of experience on technology policy, programmes and planning; the establishment of an industrial technology information bank; the provision of assistance to regional centres for technology transfer; and the publication of studies and monographs. Since 1977, UNIDO has actively sought the collaboration of other agencies in its work in this field through its Cooperative Programme of Action on Appropriate Industrial Technology. Although UNIDO has implemented more than 250 technical assistance projects concerned with establishing and strengthening national institutions within the scientific and technological infrastructure of developing countries, few of these institutions have been predominately concerned with the development and dissemination of technologies appropriate to the needs and circumstances of small entrepreneurs or the poor. Notable exceptions include UNIDO's role in establishing TCC in Ghana and the LIPI AT Unit in Indonesia, and its proposed role in strengthening the AT Unit in Lesotho. Similarly, at the international level, UNIDO has been more concerned with widening the choice of technology available to developing countries, than with providing information specifically on AT.

C. United Nations International Children's Emergency Fund (UNICEF)

Since 1974, UNICEF has been interested in promoting the use of appropriate technologies in programmes to benefit children and their families, particularly in the rural areas, and in 1975 a major initiative was taken with the creation of an AT Programme in UNICEF's East Africa Regional Office. Central to the AT Programme was the establishment of a Village Technology Unit (VTU) to demonstrate technologies appropriate to the conditions of rural communities in the region, and to provide testing and training facilities.

Following the UNICEF approach of operating through governmental channels, the VTU was established jointly with the Kenya Ministry of Housing and Social Services which incorporated the country-wide village polytechnic scheme. The VTU was established on a site next to the village polytechnic training centre, with a workshop similar to that used in the village polytechnics, to ensure that the village polytechnic instructors had proper access to the technologies.

The VTU has demonstrated a variety of low-cost water-lifting devices, water storage vessels, alternative construction techniques, improved stoves, water filters, solar dryers and crop processing technologies. This type of demonstration facility has been much criticised as resembling a museum with little capacity to transfer technologies to rural areas. The VTU was never intended to directly transfer technologies to rural communities, although it was envisaged that it would have an indirect impact on rural Kenya through training village polytechnic instructors who would transfer technologies. But although many instructors have been trained at the VTU, results have been disappointing, mainly because instructors have been unable to obtain sufficient funds to construct AT devices in their own centres and to train others.

However, there can be little doubt that the VTU is a classic demonstration/training centre. It has generated a great deal of interest in the concept of village technology in Kenya, Africa and elsewhere, and UNICEF has been asked to assist with the setting up of similar units in many parts of rural Kenya and in other countries.[30] Most of the new units concentrate on a limited number of village technologies of relevance to the immediate area in which they are located, and some have had considerable success in adapting technologies to suit local circumstances and in popularizing their use through demonstration and through training of local artisans and rural people.

D. Consultative Group on International Agricultural Research (CGIAR)

CGIAR, founded in 1971, is sponsored by the World Bank, FAO and UNDP and has twenty-five donor members. It has been notably successful in raising finance and currently funds eleven International Research Institutes devoted to agricultural research, located mainly in developing countries. Each autonomous institute has research and training functions and a library and documentation centre. Some have units to develop and transfer appropriate agricultural equipment for use by smaller farmers in developing countries.

Their experiences in bringing about widespread application of such technologies have been varied.

A successful example, which shows what can be achieved by the allocation of international funds, is the development of equipment for small paddy farmers by the Farm Machinery Unit of the International Rice Research Institute (IRRI) in the Philippines. Hardware development is preceded by a careful techno-economic analysis of traditional technology and an effort is made to mechanize selectively only those steps in which labour shortage is a problem. IRRI has found that the development of a conceptual prototype and the resulting proof of concept is only the beginning: it is necessary to adapt the prototype to the specific needs of particular manufacturers, and to provide extensive technical services until manufacturing prototypes are in production. After ten years, about 11,000 IRRI-designed machines have been commercially produced by small manufacturers in Asia, and regional industrial extension offices have been established by IRRI in Pakistan and Thailand.

By way of contrast, the International Institute for Tropical Agriculture (IITA) in Nigeria has had little success in developing and transferring appropriate equipment for small farmers. IITA's main concern is scientific research, and any hardware development work has been initiated by individual experts whose eventual departure has removed the impetus for further development and dissemination. Moreover, IITA has no extension programmes, and has had no success in bringing any of its hardware into widespread production and use.

Such internationally-funded institutions located in developing countries present the problem that their vast resources and highly-paid staff many undermine the application and confidence of the staff working in national institutions.

E. United Nations Educational, Scientific and Cultural Organisation (UNESCO)

In 1980, the Division of Technological Research and Higher Education of UNESCO organized a meeting of AT experts to advise on priority areas of work in technology for rural development. The recommendations of this meeting helped formulate the Division's current work programme, which includes among its objectives the support of existing and planned AT centres and the encouragement of linkage between such centres and rural people. UNESCO seeks to achieve these objectives in a number of ways, including the strengthening of the information delivery systems of AT centres (through improvement of library systems, training programmes, newsletters etc.); exchange programmes between AT centres; provision of consultants to develop programmes for new AT centres; and provision of information-related equipment.

In order to implement this programme, the Division is currently seeking adequate funds and the collaboration of agencies with similar objectives.

F. World Health Organisation (WHO)

In 1976, WHO established an Appropriate Technology for Health (ATH) programme aimed at promoting national self-reliance in problem-solving in primary health care delivery and at reducing the dependence of developing countries on the industrialized countries for technological support. Activities have included dissemination of information (for example, through the publication of directories of institutions working in the ATH field, and through support to agencies such as AHRTAG in collection and dissemination of information) and collaborative programmes of research to develop new appropriate health technologies (for example, development and dissemination of village-level oral rehydration techniques in collaboration with UNICEF). WHO does not appear to have become involved in encouraging the establishment of health-related AT institutions in developing countries or in strengthening the health-related activities of existing AT institutions. Indeed, health-related technologies present a noticeable gap in the activities of most AT institutions in developing countries.

G. Interim Fund on Science and Technology for Development

This new Fund was established on the recommendation of the UN Conference for Science and Technology for Development in 1979, with contributions from member governments. Part of the Fund is allocated to the support of activities relating to the generation and dissemination of technologies appropriate to the needs of rural communities in developing countries. One of the first proposed projects in this area is the provision of funds to enable RECAST in Nepal to strengthen its capacity to disseminate technologies in remote areas of the country: this project will be executed through a specialised NGO AT institution.

H. The World Bank

The World Bank has increasingly shown an awareness of the relevance of technology choice in its operations. The Office of the Adviser for Science and Technology has responsibility for advising on the technology content of all World Bank projects, and has strong links with the specialized AT institutions (and, in particular with VITA, which has seconded a staff member to the Office).

Although, instances of specific support to AT institutions are rare, the World Bank has recently given assistance to Las Gaviotas in Columbia, and contributes to the Consultative Group on International Agricultural Research. It has also maintained a technology unit in Kenya to undertake research and development work in the construction of rural access roads.[31]

I. Commonwealth Secretariat

The Division of Food Production and Rural Development (FPRD) of the Commonwealth Secretariat is actively involved in the promotion and transfer of suitable technology (in particular, small-scale agricultural and agro-industrial equipment) to and between developing countries of the Commonwealth. In this, it acts as a clearing house for identifying sources of funds and expertise for projects and for referring technical enquiries. It also organizes and funds meetings, study tours and training.

The FPRD Division's most significant achievement in respect to AT institutions has been the organization and funding of a number of regional Rural Technology Meetings".[32] As the Commonwealth Secretariat works through the governments of Commonwealth countries, most of the participants at the meetings represent government ministries and agencies. These meetings are intended to generate follow-up action in the countries and regions concerned, which can be assisted by the Commonwealth Secretariat and other agencies. Recommendations for follow-up action have been directed towards the establishment of National Appropriate Technology Committees, the establishment of Regional Appropriate Technology Committess, and programmes for the transfer and exchange of AT equipment and personnel between countries in the region.

Limited success in establishing committees is in part due to the FPRD Division's approach. First, its agricultural and rural development orientation means that government representatives at the meetings come mainly from ministries involved in these areas, and NATCs, when formed, tend to be established within, or seen as the creation of, these ministries. This limits the NATC's access and involvement in other sectors of the economy and its ability to co-ordinate AT activities on a national level. Second, the FPRD Division's staff have limited capacity to provide the on-going advice and assistance necessary to turn NATC recommendations into action, and other specialized AT institutions have to be relied on to carry out this function.

J. Transnational Network for Appropriate Technology (TRANET)

At the 1976 Habitat Conference, representatives of several NGO AT institutions determined that a mechanism was needed to strengthen the links between them. TRANET was the result, the only non-governmental/non-UN AT initiative at the international level.

Initially, information on the publications and activities of the various AT institutions was provided through a voluntary clearing house and quarterly newsletter. Inevitably, the need for core funding to continue and expand activities required the formalization of the network, and in 1979 TRANET was registered as a non-profit organization, with a Board of Directors composed of representatives from AT institutions world-wide and a secretariat in the USA. In expanding its activities, TRANET faces the problem of identifying work that does not duplicate the efforts of its member institutions and at the same time maintains the original objectives of strengthening links between them.

K. Summary

Some international agencies such as UNIDO have held a broad definition of appropriate technology, taking it as technology appropriate to a country as a whole rather than technology appropriate to the needs and circumstances of the rural and urban poor. Others such as ILO and UNICEF have a more basic needs approach in defining the concept of appropriate technology and the functions of AT Institutions.

The international agencies have focussed on the transfer of technological information to developing countries, through the establishment of information clearing houses and establishment and strengthening of technology transfer centres, and on the encouragement of the formation of committees and councils which advise governments on technology policy and co-ordinate technology activities. Less emphasis has been placed on the establishment of mechanisms to link research and development agencies with commercial production units and/or the intended beneficiaries of their research. The ILO's Rural Technology Centre programme is aimed at this aspect, however, and UNICEF's initiative in Kenya has also considered this aspect through its proposed emphasis on disseminating technologies through the village polytechnic system.

V. SUMMARY ANALYSIS, CONCLUSIONS, AND RECOMMENDATIONS FOR FURTHER WORK

Over the past twenty years, the institutions in the AT movement have been concerned with bringing the concept of appropriate technology to the forefront of development thinking, partly through the collection and dissemination of information, and partly through practical research and development, testing and demonstration at the pilot project level.

It cannot be denied that the concept of AT has caught on but, although the conceptualists have made rapid progress in a very few years, the headway they have made is at risk unless more is done quickly to present proof of concept. Many of the AT institutions in the developing countries were established, in part, to provide such proof through practical work. Although they have done much to bring AT to its present status, examples of projects which have taken technologies beyond the pilot stage into widespread production and use are very thin on the ground. This remains the case, moreover, even after the considerable support given to the AT movement over the past five years by governments and international agencies.

Advice and assistance are increasingly being requested on ways of identifying and overcoming the institutional and other non-technical problems faced in applying AT. The purpose of this study was broadly to review, classify and analyse the experiences of selected AT institutions to determine to what extent existing information could provide answers to institutional questions, to identify gaps in institutional knowledge and experience, and to clarify some of the issues besetting the AT movement. Recommendations could then be made on the further work required to increase the institutional information available, to fill the gaps, and to resolve the issues, with the eventual aim of being able to provide better institutional advice and assistance to those concerned with the development and implementation of appropriate technology.

There are basically four categories of people who ask questions about the institutional aspects of appropriate technology.

- (a) governments in developing countries who are interested in AT and want to know how they should promote it or how they could make their existing mechanism for promoting AT more effective;
- (b) people outside the governmental sector in developing countries who are interested in AT and want to know how they could best promote its application, or who have established an AT institution and want to know how to overcome the difficulties they are experiencing;
- (c) people outside the governmental sector in developed countries who are experiencing difficulties with their existing AT initiatives and want to know how to overcome them;
- (d) bilateral and multilateral aid agencies and international non-governmental organizations who want to know if the type of programmes and services they provide to AT institutions are effective.

The circumstances and resources of those in each of these categories differ significantly, and some of the problems they face and the questions they ask vary accordingly. The provision of advice to each of these categories thus has to be based on analysis of the experiences within the same category.

Governments in developing countries interested in the promotion of AT have a number of options open to them. At the institutional level, they can establish a National Appropriate Technology Committee or an Appropriate Technology Development Centre. At the operational levels, they can initiate pilot projects for the application of AT in a localized area; give direct support in cash or kind to other agencies working on AT; vet development projects for the appropriateness of their technology input; assess economic policies with respect to their effect on the development and dissemination of AT and alter these accordingly; or a combination of these measures. These operational measures are ofter included among the functions of NATCs or ATDCs, but some can be carried out without establishing either.

Experience suggests that it is relatively easy to establish a NATC, since it requires no special commitment of staff or funds and only passive support. However, it will have little influence on government policy unless it has a secretariat with executive powers located in a key position in the government structure. It will have difficulty in translating its ideas into action without an 'action arm', with expert technical staff, funds and active support, which can implement projects in collaboration with other agencies.

National ATDCs, in contrast, are expected to be involved in project implementation, and their establishment (with staff and funds) requires a real commitment by government. The ways in which they work, the problems they encounter, and their effectiveness in meeting their ovjectives depend on a variety of factors, in particular their institutional affiliation (whether they are linked to a parastatal, an extension ministry, a planning ministry, or a research and development institute) and their degree of institutional independence. Little in depth is known about the impact of these institutional factors, and it is difficult to assess which institutional arrangement would be suitable for a situation and the consequences of such decisions. Enough is known of National Appropriate Technology Committees to allow the preparation of guidelines covering the circumstances where a NATC could be established and its terms of reference, organization and operational procedures. Such guidelines would be for use by governments planning to establish or improve a NATC. However, there are serious gaps in knowledge with regard to national Appropriate Technology Development Centres. Further work is needed on the institutional factors and on the strengths and weaknesses of national ATDCs based variously on coordination, research and development, and extension. Guidelines could then be prepared for use by governments planning to establish or improve a national

ATDC.

People outside the governmental sector in developing countries also have a number of options open to them. Those working within a university (or other academic/research institute) or a non-governmental organization can establish an AT Committee; however, experience indicates that committees outside government have serious problems and fail to evolve. Those working within a university can establish an affiliated, independent ATDC. Those within a NGO can establish an ATDC or can enter into a cooperative agreement with a university. Experience indicates that university groups have had considerable success in developing and transferring new technologies to small entrepreneurs but less success in transferring technologies to rural communities. On the other hand, NGO groups have often had success with rural technology programmes, both in establishing small rural industries and in improving the living standards in rural communities.

Those working within a university can also seek to bring about appropriate changes in teaching curricula and/or provide technological inputs to existing programmes of rural development agencies. These measures are often included among the functions of AT Committees of ATDCs but can be undertaken without establishing either.

Enough is known of the nature and problems of university and NGO AT institutions to allow the provision of some general advice to others planning to establish or improve such institutions. However, although problems have been identified, few specific and no general solutions have been found for some key problems. These problems are considered later in this section in a more general context. Clearly, there is a need to study these problems further and to find solutions to them, so that more helpful advice and assistance can be provided.

In developed countries, people outside the governmental sector can contribute to the development and dissemination of AT in developing countries in a number of ways. Those working within a university (or other academic/research institute) can establish an ATDC: however, the few such centres that have been set up have had difficulty in developing a methodology for working with overseas Those in universities can also assist other AT institutions in their countries to answer technical enquiries from developing countries. They can also work towards the establishment of AT components in science and engineering courses: this is particularly useful, in that it influences the interests and skills of future generations of technologists, many of whom come from and return to developing countries.

NGO AT institutions in developed countries were initially set up to provide general AT information, answer technical enquiries and encourage AT institutions in developing countries, but as the AT institutions in developing countries have increased in number and maturity, the task has become that of finding ways to respond to increasingly complex technical and institutional enquiries. Some of the developed country organizations have taken the approach of providing in-depth technical assistance by working on collaborative projects with overseas institutions: others have tried to improve their capacity to respond by setting up information networking systems. Experience indicates that the collaborative project approach is more promising, although it has proved difficult to obtain the staff necessary for this approach and to develop a methodology for doing it well. The issue of how to assist overseas organizations through institutional advice remains largely unresolved.

Thus as the AT movement has evolved, problems of a different and more complex nature have emerged. The challenge for AT organizations in developed countries is to determine and develop methods of responding effectively to enquiries and requests for assistance arising from these problems. As yet, there are no well-developed guidelines to assist them to meet this challenge, and further work will be necessary to fill this knowledge gap.

Bilateral and multilateral aid agencies interested in the development of AT also have a variety of options. They can provide AT institutions in developing countries with financial and logistic support, information services, and/or direct technical assistance. They can organize meetings and undertake studies to create a more favourable environment for AT in developing countries. Bilateral agencies can establish and support specialized AT institutions in their own countries Multilateral agencies can encourage the establishment of regional or international AT institutions, and give them on-going support. Non-specialist NGOs and overseas volunteer organizations can also play a role by provision of financial and logistic support and volunteer staff.

Bilateral aid agencies which have established their own AT institutions have tended to concentrate on the transfer of technical information and hardware from their own countries. Others have concentrated largely on the provision of financial support to government sponsored/controlled AT institutions in developing countries. Multilateral aid agencies have concentrated mainly on technology transfer through establishing international technical clearing houses and encouraging and assisting developing country governments to establish national and regional technology transfer centres. There has also been some involvement in research and development through the establishment of international research and development institutes and through provision of experts as part of technical assistance: however, there has been little emphasis on field testing of prototypes or the linking of research and development institutes with commercial firms, or with the intended beneficiaries of research. In contrast with bilateral and multilateral aid agencies, international NGOs and volunteers agencies have concentrated on assisting university and non-governmental AT institutions.

There is insufficient information available to assess the value of these various assistance measures: the existing evidence, however, indicates that the impact in terms of bringing AT into widespread sustained application has not as yet been commensurate with the resources expended. The roles that these aid agencies could or should play are still unclear and warrant further investigation.

Although by far the largest number of enquiries on the application of AT come from the agencies already considered there are also a number of private industrial enterprises who are interested in AT for commercial (rather than philanthropic) reasons. This interest has been increasing recently as they realize (in part because of the work of existing AT institutions) the value of opening up markets in poor communities. It is unknown what roles they could or should play in the application of AT: questions relating to this are now being raised, and it is important that attempts are made to provide answers.

In reviewing the experiences of the selected AT institutions and support agencies, certain themes and problem areas have been identified which appear to have little relationship to the characteristics and location of particular institutions but rather appear inherent in the nature of the work of applying appropriate technology. These 'crosscutting' themes and problem areas are considered here.

A major problem area is that of personnel: AT institutions experience three particular difficulties. First, because of the youth of the AT movement and the general lack of experience in the application of AT, it is difficult to find people who know how to establish and manage an AT institution. The usual approach in setting up an AT institution is to copy what others have done and, since there is little published information relating to the theory and practice of establishing and managing AT institutions, the chosen option is usually to establish close working relationships with the more established organizations which provide assistance. However, the latter are unable to cope adequately with more than a handfull of newcomers, which leaves the majority to fend largely for themselves. There is thus a strong argument for researching and publishing guidelines on how to establish and manage an AT institution, and for establishing suitable specialized management training courses.

Second, given the low prestige attached to AT research and development work and the budgetary constraints of most AT institutions, it is difficult to attract sufficiently qualified technologists away from more prestigious and lucrative positions. One favoured approach is to use expatriate personnel provided through technical assistance programmes or volunteer schemes, but this is only a stop-gap measure which does little to solve the problem of attracting qualified indigenous engineers. Attempts have been made by small groups of engineering teachers within universities to interest their colleagues and students in AT, and by governments to interest existing research and development institutes, but these have had little impact. Continued efforts of this nature are necessary, but the situation is unlikely to change significantly until the rewards attached to working on appropriate technology match those of working on conventional technologies

Third, the personnel of AT institutions are scientists and engineers, most of whom have had no training or experience in commerce, economics or sociology. This lack of non-technical expertise often means that vital aspects of the work (such as needs assessment and socio-economic constraints on the adoption of new technology) can be overlooked. The assistance of other agencies can be sought, but the staff of an AT institution will be unlikely to attach much priority to securing this input unless they recognize its importance. It is unclear whether this capacity could be best strengthened in AT institutions by recruiting more non-technological staff or by training engineering staff so that they can identify non-technological constraints to their work and seek assistance accordingly.

Another major problem faced by AT institutions is funding. As governments, international development agencies and others have become more interested in AT, funding has increased significantly, including the direct funding of AT institutions. However, the problem appears to be not so much one of lack of funds per se, as one of securing funds for specific aspects of the work: while funds are made available for the transfer of technologies and technical information and to support research and development, very little is made available for the critical stage of field testing prototypes and processes. Widespread application of AT requires the funding of all stages in the process.

These appear to be two factors contributing to this problem. First, the support agencies are either unable, because of their rules and regulations, or unwilling, because of the uncertainties and risks involved, to provide funds for all aspects of work requested by an AT institution. The tendency is to fund the parts of the project which relate to information and research and development in which there has been more experience and for which the input requirements and expected outputs can be more accurately estimated. This mismatching of funds contributes to the observable trend for AT institutions to attempt to earn income of their own and thus have more freedom of action in addressing priority tasks as they perceive them. Second, some of the AT institutions may be unaware of the importance of all of the stages in the process of applying appropriate technology, and consequently seek funds for only those aspects of their work for which funds are known to be available rather than the less well-tried and understood aspects. This is compounded by lack of experience with the latter aspects and the consequent difficulty in preparing a project proposal to obtain funds for them. This issue of matching available funds to specific activities requires further investigation from both the standpoint of the support agencies and the AT institutions themselves.

Another common theme is the importance of setting up an AT institution in such a way that it can effectively carry out its objectives. Experience indicates that certain factors (such as lack of full-time staff, inadequate independence, or an inappropriate institutional affiliation) can drastically reduce the ability of an AT institution to have any impact. Objectives are often set without any attention being given to the structure or institutional affiliation of the organisation expected to meet the objectives, and experience shows that if structure or affiliation are wrong, then simply pouring in money and other resources will be of little value. Moreover, once an organization is established, changes are difficult to make and the assistance needed to do so is difficult to obtain It appears essential that guidelines are developed for the organizational structure and institutional affiliation of AT institutions.

AT institutions also face problems of developing a suitable methodology for achieving their objectives. The process of applying appropriate technology is a highly complex one, involving: identifying needs and potential markets; seeking out appropriate technological solutions; adapting existing technologies or developing new ones; undertaking pilot operations to prove technical feasibility and economic viability; and transferring new processes and products to local entrepreneurs and users, complete with necessary back-up. Experience indicates that the task of taking technologies to widespread production and use defeats most AT institutions, with many projects progressing no further than the development of a prototype. Problems arise in two particular ways. First, insufficient care may be taken at the crucial stage of identifying needs and markets. Thus many laboratory prototypes are too expensive for the intended users or are in some other way inappropriate, and consequently there is a reluctance to undertake the necessary field work to correct the situation, and a tendency to abandon them and try again. Second, even if a truly appropriate technology is developed, there is a tendency by AT institutions to assume that it will sell itself. This is rarely the case, and field trials are usually necessary to prove viability before low income groups will invest in new technologies and create an effective demand.

Experience suggests that the time and resources needed to go through the full process are frequently not committed, and very little of significance consequently results. There are a few AT institutions that have developed a methodology to get beyond prototype development, but these are a very small minority: their experiences should be examined in order to prepare guidelines for the assistance of others.

Finally, the effectiveness of AT institutions depends upon external factors which are largely outside their control: in particular, government policy with regard to taxation/subsidies and imports/industrial licensing can have a strong impact on the development and dissemination of AT for reasons independent of the technologies. Although AT institutions can generally do little about such policy factors, a strong NATC may be able to effect specific policies, while an ATDC may be able to prove the validity of changing a policy affecting a specific technology; there are, however, very few recorded cases of this happening.

Given the magnitude of the tasks involved in the identification and development of suitable policies for the promotion of AT in various countries, there is a need for more empirical research on the impact of various policies and combinations of policies to be able to develop guidelines so that governments and AT institutions can better understand the interaction of policies and appropriate technology.

The five cross-cutting themes and problem areas considered are crucial to an understanding of the present state of the AT movement, and they require further priority attention if the ultimate aim of widespread production and use of appropriate technologies is to be realized. Studies of specific AT institutions can help to identify some of the problems and suggest ways of overcoming them in certain circumstances, but some of the problems are of such a fundamental nature that research of a more comprehensive kind will be needed.

The general conclusions and recommendations made here are based on a selective sample of AT institutions, and consequently coverage is weaker on some model types and certain geographical areas. These knowledge gaps will have to be filled before more definite conclusions can be reached and more definitive recommendations can be made.

Some of the recommendations for further work presented here form the major part of the work programme of ITDG's Appropriate Technology Institutions Unit. However, it is not within ITDG's capabilities to follow up on all of the recommendations for further work. Other appropriate agencies may be prepared to undertake some of this work, either in conjunction with ITDG or independently.

NOTES

1. The pioneer AT institutions of particular importance were the Intermediate Technology Development Group (ITDG) in UK, and Volunteers in Technical Assistance (VITA) in USA.
2. These include: Holtermann, S., *Intermediate Technology in Ghana: The Experience of Kumasi University's Technology Consultancy Centre* (ITIS, Rugby, 1979); UNICEF, *Appropriate Technology for Basic Services* (UNICEF EARO, Nairobi, 1980); Carr, M., *Developing Small-scale Industries in India: The Experience of the Birla Institute of Technology's Small Industry Scheme* (IT Publications, London, 1981).
3. These include: Canadian Freedom from Hunger Foundation, *A Handbook on Appropriate Technology*, Section C.4: Groups Involved in Appropriate Technology Development (CFHF, Ottawa, 1976); Commonwealth Secretariat, *Rural Technology in the Commonwealth: A Directory of Organisations.* (CS Food Production and Rural Development Division, London, 1980); Jequier, N., *Appropriate Technology Directory* (Development Centre of the OECD, Paris, 1979); Reddy, A.K.N., 'National and Regional Technology Groups and Institutions', in Bhalla, A.S. (ed.), *Towards Global Action for Appropriate Technology* (ILO, Geneva, 1979); Singer, H., *Technologies for Basic Needs,* Annex B: Institutions Dealing with Appropriate Technology (ILO, Geneva, 1978); Transnational Network for Appropriate Technology, various issues of the *TRANET Newsletter;* UNEP, *Institutions and Individuals Active in Environmentally Sound and Appropriate Technologies* (UNEP, Nairobi, 1978); Mathur, B., *International Directory of Appropriate Technology Resources* (VITA, Washington, 1978).
4. The Appendix lists AT Institutions and other agencies

referred to in the text.
5. A number of categorizations have been made by others. These are included in: Herrera, A.O., *The Generation and Dissemination of Appropriate Technologies in Developing Countries,* Working paper No. 51 (ILO, Geneva, 1979); Reddy, A.K.N., 'National and Regional Technology Groups and Institutions' in Bhalla, A.S. (ed), *Towards Global Action for Appropriate Technology* (ILO, Geneva, 1979); Jequier, N., *The World of Appropriate Technology: A Quantitative Analysis* (Development Centre of the OECD, Paris, unpublished draft).
6. For example, Malawi has established two of five planned sub-committees, dealing with agricultural machinery, rural industry, social technology, energy, and agricultural production.
7. Other government sponsored/controlled AT Development Centres not discussed here include the Product Development Unit of Kenya Industrial Estates, the Gujarat State Rural Technology Institute in India, and the Appropriate Technology Development Organisation in Pakistan.
8. The original proposal to establish the Lesotho ATDC was made by ITDG at the request of the Lesotho Government in 1976.
9. The process of establishing the Botswana Technology Centre began in earnest in 1977, and primarily involved ITDG, the European Economic Community, the Botswana Development Corporation and the Ministry of Finance.
10. The Botswana Government commissioned ITDG to search for a suitable director, and selected the director from the short-list submitted by ITDG.
11. ATDI is an autonomous unit attached to the University with a Governing Board made up of representatives from the University, SPATF, the Office of Village Development, and the Melanesian Council of Churches (which provides financial support).
12. RECAST is one of three research centres responsible to a Managing Committee of the National University, chaired by the Vice-Chancellor of the University with members from relevant government ministries.

13. Funding has been sought from the United Nations Interim Fund on Science and Technology for Development.
14. The ATDCs of Lesotho, Botswana, Papua New Guinea and Tanzania have made extensive use of expatriate personnel. National counterparts have taken over in all but Botswana (but expatriates are expected to return in the restructured Lesotho ATDC). In the Columbian and Nepalese ATDCs expatriates have been used only on short-term technical projects (but expatriate personnel are expected in the restructured Nepalese ATDC).
15. Other academic/research institute AT Development Centres, not discussed here, include the Technology Development Advisory Unit of the University of Zambia, the Technology Development and Consultancy Centre at the University of Mauritius, the AT Cell at Allahabad Polytechnic in India, the AT Cell at the Indian Institute of Technology in New Delhi, and the AT Cell at the Indian Institute of Technology in Bombay.
16. This helped to introduce a significant change in attitude, whereby the graduates of a university began to see themselves as job creators rather than job seekers.
17. Some of these problems stem from the time when ATDI was a fully-controlled unit of the University, and may be expected to decrease following its recent establishment as an autonomous institute.
18. In the first three years of the programme, CEMAT trainees built (for payment) 1,800 stoves in the three regions where courses had been organized.
19. Although ATDA's development of competitive small-scale sugar plants required some ten years work, the technology has now become accepted and widely implemented. This demonstrates the validity of this approach.
20. Other NGO AT Development Centres, not discussed herein, include the Malindi Rural Training Centre in Malawi, the Rural Industries Innovation Centre in Botswana, the Thaba Tseka Integrated Rural Development Project in Lesotho, and the Appropriate Technology Group in Sri Lanka.
21. Of particular interest is CEMAT's establishment of a

profit-making subsidiary consultancy firm to undertake work throughout Latin America.
22. These include major renewable energy projects in Botswana, Lesotho, and Malawi.
23. SATIS does not provide financial assistance to groups to convert to its system, and other support agencies have shown little interest in providing funds for this purpose. An exception is GATE, which has allocated £20,000 a year to collaborating agencies for this purpose.
24. The evaluation also recommended changes in structure and policy-making procedures.
25. An exception is ATI, which does not engage in projects but provides financial and logistic support to increase the capacity of overseas institutions.
26. Universities offering degrees or courses in appropriate technology include the University of Edinburgh, the University of Reading, the University of Warwick, and the University of East Anglia in the UK, and Washington University, Arizona State University, and Stevens Institute of Technology in the USA.
27. Others include the Georgia Institute of Technology and the University of New Mexico in the USA.
28. These include the Botswana Technology Centre, SRAT in Upper Volta, and the Liklik Buk Information Centre in Papua New Guinea.
29. ITDG was heavily involved in the establishment of ATDO (Pakistan), ATDA (India), ATG (Sri Lanka), TCC (Ghana), BTC (Botswana) and other AT institutions in developing countries.
30. Village technology units have been set up in Lesotho, Swaziland, Uganda, Ethiopia, Ghana, Bangladesh and Guyana.
31. The Kenyan rural roads project has extended over ten years and has shown that with proper organization, good supervision, and well-designed hand-tools, it is technically feasible and economically possible to build rural access roads and dig canals without using heavy equipment.
32. Regional Rural Technology Meetings have been held in East Africa, West Africa and the South Pacific, and a meeting is planned for the Caribbean.

APPENDIX: APPROPRIATE TECHNOLOGY INSTITUTIONS AND SUPPORT AGENCIES REVIEWED OR CITED

I. AT INSTITUTIONS IN DEVELOPING COUNTRIES

National Appropriate Technology Committees
Science and Technology Committee, Guyana.
Standing Committee for Appropriate Technology, Indonesia
National Appropriate Technology Committee, Kenya
National Appropriate Technology Committee, Malawi
National Association for Appropriate Technology, Sierra Leone
National Appropriate Technology Committee, Tanzania
National Committee for Appropriate Technology, Zambia

Government Appropriate Technology Development Centres and Initiatives
Botswana Technology Centre, Botswana
Centro 'Las Gaviotas', Columbia
Servicia Nacional de Aprendizaje (SENA), Columbia
Institute of Applied Science and Technology (IAST), Guyana
Appropriate Technology Unit, Basotho Enterprises Development Corporation, Lesotho
Rural Technology Institute, Gujarat State, India
Product Development Unit, Kenya Industrial Estates, Kenya
Research Centre for Applied Science and Technology (RECAST), Nepal
Appropriate Technology Development Organisations, Pakistan
South Pacific Appropriate Technology Foundation (SPATF), Papua New Guinea
Arusha Appropriate Technology Project (AATP), Tanzania

University Appropriate Technology Development Centres
Universidad de los Andes, Columbia
Technology Consultancy Centre (TCC), University of Science and Technology, Kumasi, Ghana

Appropriate Technology Cell, Allahabad Polytechnic, India
Cell for Application of Science and Technology in Rural Areas (ASTRA), Indian Institute of Management, Bangalore, India
Appropriate Technology Cell, Indian Institute of Technology, Bombay, India
Appropriate Technology Cell, Indian Institute of Technology, New Delhi, India
Small Industry Research, Training and Development Organisation (SIRTDO), Birla Institute of Technology, Ranchi, India
Development Technology Centre (DTC), Bandung Institute of Technology, Indonesia
Technology Development and Consultancy Centre (TDCC), University of Mauritius, Mauritius
Appropriate Technology Development Institute (ATDI), University of Technology, Lae, Papua New Guinea
Advisory Services Unit for Technology Research and Development (ASTRAD), Fourah Bay College, Sierra Leone
Technology Development Advisory Unit (TDAU), University of Zambia, Zambia

NGO Appropriate Technology Development Centres
Rural Industries Innovation Centre (RIIC), Botswana
Centro de Estudios Mesoamericanos y de Technologia Apropiada (CEMAT), Guatemala
Appropriate Technology Development Association (ATDA), Lucknow, India
Dian Desa, Indonesia
Thaba Tseka Integrated Rural Development Project, Lesotho
Malindi Rural Training Centre, Malawi
Small Farm Equipment Unit, Tikonko Agricultural Extension Centre, Sierra Leone
Appropriate Technology Group (ATG), Sri Lanka
Society for Research and Application of Technology (SRAT), Upper Volta

Regional Institutions and Initiatives
Appropriate Technology Referral Service (ATRS), Christian

Action for Development in the Caribbean (CADEC), Barbados
UN/ESCAP Regional Centre for Technology Transfer (RCTT), Bangalore, India
UN/ECA African Regional Centre for Technology (ARCT), Dakar, Senegal
Technology Relay, Environment Development Training Programme (ENDA), Dakar, Senegal
Technonet/Asian Alliance of Appropriate Technology Practitioners (AAATP), Singapore
Comite de Coordinacion y Promocion de Technologia Apropiada (COCOP) — moving secretariat

II AT INSTITUTIONS IN DEVELOPED COUNTRIES

Government Institutions
Group de Recherche et Échange Technologique (GRET), France
German Appropriate Technology Exchange (GATE), Germany
TOOL Foundation, The Netherlands
Intermediate Technology Industrial Services (ITIS), UK
Tropical Products Institute (TPI), UK
Appropriate Technology International (ATI), USA

University Institutions
Brace Research Institute, McGill University, Canada
Centre for Appropriate Technology (CAT), University of Delft, The Netherlands
Appropriate Technology Department, University of Eindhoven, The Netherlands
Georgia Institute of Technology, USA
University of New Mexico, USA

NGO Institutions
Association for Appropriate Technology in Developing Countries (ATOL), Belgium
Collectif D'Échanges pour la Technologie Appropriée (COTA), Belgium

Swiss Centre for Appropriate Technology (SKAT), Switzerland
Appropriate Health Resources and Technologies Action Group (AHRTAG), UK
Intermediate Technology Development Group (ITDG), UK
Volunteers in Technical Assistance (VITA), USA

International Institutions and Networks
International Institute for Tropical Agriculture (IITA), Ibadan, Nigeria
International Rice Research Institute (IRRI), Manila, The Philippines
Transnational Network for Appropriate Technology (TRANET), USA

III. SUPPORT AGENCIES

Bilateral Donor Agencies
Canadian International Development Agency (CIDA), Canada
Ministere de la Cooperation et du Developpment, France
Ministry of Economic Cooperation, German Agency for Technical Cooperation (GTZ), Germany
Ministry of Foreign Affairs, Technical Assistance Department The Netherlands
Ministry of Foreign Affairs, Department of External Aid, New Zealand
Swedish International Development Agency (SIDA), Sweden
Overseas Development Administration (ODA), UK
United States Agency for International Development (USAID), USA

Multilateral Donor Agencies
Commonwealth Secretariat
Consultative Group on International Agricultural Research (CGIAR)
Interim Fund on Science and Technology for Development (IFSTD)
International Labour Organisation (ILO)
United Nations Education, Scientific and Cultural Organis-

ation (UNESCO)
United Nations Industrial Development Organisation (UNIDO)
United Nations International Children's Emergency Fund (UNICEF)
The World Bank
World Health Organisation (WHO)

International NGOs
Canadian Freedom From Hunger Foundation, Canada
Bread for the World, Germany
Freidrich Neumann Foundation, Germany
ICCO, The Netherlands
NOVIB, The Netherlands
Christian Aid, UK
OXFAM, UK
Rockefeller Foundation, USA

Overseas Volunteer Organizations
Canadian University Service Overseas (CUSO), Canada
Voluntary Service Overseas (VSO), UK
International Voluntary Services (IVS), USA
The Peace Corps, USA
Volunteers in Asia (VIA), USA

The ITDG Occasional Papers Series

1. Marilyn Carr, **Appropriate Technology and Rural Industrialisation** . . . .
2. Derek Miles, **Appropriate Technology for Rural Development: The ITDG Experience** . . .
3. John Davis, **New Directions for Technology: The Tawney Lecture 1981** . . . .
4. George McRobie & Marilyn Carr, **Mass Production or Production by the Masses?** . . . . . .
5. Marilyn Carr, **Women and Appropriate Technology: Two Essays** . . . .
6. Alan Bollard, **Industrial Employment through Appropriate Technology** . . . . . .
7. Richard Whitcombe & Marilyn Carr, **Appropriate Technology Institutions: A Review** . . .

www.ingramcontent.com/pod-product-compliance
Ingram Content Group UK Ltd.
Pitfield, Milton Keynes, MK11 3LW, UK
UKHW021839140426
5217IPUK00022B/1516

9 781853 391514